SOCIAL SCIENCE SEMINAR SERIES

Raymond H. Muessig and Vincent R. Rogers, Editors

THE VOLUMES AND THE AUTHORS

The Study of Anthropology, Pertti J. Pelto

Political Science: An Informal Overview, Francis J. Sorauf

Geography: Its Scope and Spirit, Jan O. M. Broek

Sociology: The Study of Man in Society, Caroline B. Rose

The Nature and the Study of History, Henry Steele Commager

Economics and Its Significance, Richard S. Martin and
 Reuben G. Miller

THE CONSULTANTS FOR THE SERIES

Anthropology, George D. Spindler

Political Science, Charles S. Hyneman

Geography, Jan O. M. Broek

Sociology, Arnold M. Rose

History, Henry Steele Commager

Economics, Kenneth E. Boulding

ECONOMICS
AND ITS SIGNIFICANCE

Richard S. Martin
Reuben G. Miller
Department of Economics
University of Massachusetts

Kenneth E. Boulding, *Consultant*
Department of Economics
The University of Michigan

With a Concluding Chapter Suggesting Methods
for Elementary and Secondary Teachers
by **Raymond H. Muessig** *and* **Vincent R. Rogers**

CHARLES E. MERRILL BOOKS, INC.   Columbus, Ohio

PRINTED IN THE UNITED STATES OF AMERICA

Social Science Seminar Series

Edited by Raymond H. Muessig
and Vincent R. Rogers

The Social Science Seminar Series presents scholarly viewpoints on and information about history, geography, political science, economics, sociology, and anthropology. This social science material is complemented by creative and practical methods, tailored to each of the individual fields, for elementary and secondary teachers.

One assumption built into these six volumes is that the social studies program in our schools should reflect more faithfully and sensitively the social sciences from which it is derived. It is imperative, then, that social scientists contribute their suggestions regarding over-all content selection problems in the social studies.

A second premise inherent in the Social Science Seminar Series is that professional educators are responsible for translating appropriate social science substance into meaningful and enriching learning experiences for children and youth. In their contacts with the editors of this Series, the contributing social scientists repeatedly made the point that they could discuss their disciplines only as they saw them and not in the light of what should be done with them in the schools. It is the professional educator—thoroughly prepared and broadly experienced in thinking about and coping with educational theories, problems, and practices—who must weld a framework that will support understandings, skills, attitudes, and appreciations drawn from or tied to the social science disciplines. It is the educator, too, who must decide what can and should be taught at various grade levels and how this subject matter might be conveyed, buttressed, and assessed by a myriad of suitable methods, materials, resources, and evaluative processes.

There is a critical need in both pre-service and in-service teacher education programs for up-to-date, clear, stimulating material concerned with recent developments in the social sciences. Teachers should see these disciplines as spheres of continuing scientific study and inquiry, rather than as hardened, static, sterile bodies of accumulated fact. Further, they must obtain a more sophisticated grasp of the goals, scope, importance, and interpretation of these fields as well as some understanding of the concerns faced by those working in a given field. The Social Science Seminar Series encourages and assists teachers at all instructional levels to critically examine their purposes in and approaches to the teaching of specific areas of content fundamentally related to the disciplines treated.

With this perspective in mind, the editors of the Series suggested that each of the contributing social scientists ask himself what his field really does contain that professional educators should consider teaching to youngsters. Each author was asked to describe the nature of his field; to trace briefly its history, development, and maturation; and to look at its unique methods of working as well as those procedures shared with other social sciences and related fields. Most importantly, each specialist was requested to select out of mountains of data a series of fundamental, compelling ideas that have emerged from his field.

In each volume of the Social Science Seminar Series, the editors have written a final chapter to accompany the discussions and analyses of the social scientists. The editors have *not* attempted to build an overarching theory of social studies education; rather, they have concentrated upon specific, functional classroom methods. The concluding chapters in this Series, therefore, do not present a total program, a master theory, a blanket plan of attack, or an endorsement of the proposals of any single group endeavoring to improve social studies instruction. The generalizations the editors have chosen to illustrate should not be viewed as the basis for a course or sequence of offerings. The ideas they have introduced transcend particular topics, units, themes, or curricula. Careful exposure to them can support many learnings. The editors have not dealt at this time with *why, how much, where,* and *when* questions regarding the place of individual social sciences in the social studies family today or tomorrow. As they see it, each social science can be taught by itself in breadth or depth, woven into existing scope and sequence patterns for development or supplementary purposes, or assigned manifold roles in some yet-to-be-developed curriculum design.

Space limitations have not permitted the exhaustive treatment of a single idea, problem, or approach drawn from each of the social sciences represented. Instead, the editors have suggested a number of procedures that could be used or adapted for use in a variety of elementary and secondary school situations. It is not intended that the techniques offered in the Series be employed in a one-a-day, isolated, disjointed, decontextualized fashion. A superficial flitting from one major insight to another would have little meaning for students and would possess limited retention or transfer value. It is not expected that pupils will comprehend abstract generalizations in a definitive sense after an occasional lesson or two. The editors believe that global ideas should be approached, discovered, introduced, developed, and confirmed in different ways and contexts and at increased levels of complexity throughout the school years. They have taken into account the fact that it takes time, patience, and systematic organization to build durable learning.

The Social Science Seminar Series, then, should function as a point of embarkation—inspiring and challenging readers to keep abreast of developments in the social sciences and in social studies education.

Preface

In his presidential address delivered at the Sixty-third Annual Meeting of the American Economic Association in Chicago, Frank H. Knight, Morton D. Hull Distinguished Service Professor Emeritus of Social Sciences and Philosophy at the University of Chicago, combined witticism with profundity in these two comments:

> . . . A humorist once popular in this country stated my favorite "principle" in education: "It ain't ignorance that does the most damage, it's knowin' so derned much that ain't so."
>
> . . . If free society is to exist, the electorate must be informed and must have and use economic and political intelligence and, of course, possess the moral qualities actually needful. . . .[1]

Paul A. Samuelson, Professor of Economics at the Massachusetts Institute of Technology, has sounded a note of warning which might be coupled with Knight's words:

> The plain truth is this, and it is known to anyone who has looked into the matter: The science of economics does not provide simple answers to complex social problems. . . .[2]

And Alvin H. Hansen, Lucius N. Littauer Professor of Political Economy, Emeritus, at Harvard University, has provided us with a third statement, which is an appropriate addition to those already cited. He writes: "We have learned how to make a living; we have still to learn how to live."[3]

---

[1] "The Role of Principles in Economics and Politics," in Frank H. Knight, *On the History and Method of Economics: Selected Essays* (Chicago: Phoenix Books, The University of Chicago Press, 1963), pp. 256 and 273.
[2] "Public Responsibility for Growth and Stability," in Edmund S. Phelps (ed.), *The Goal of Economic Growth* (New York: W. W. Norton & Company, Inc., 1962), p. 38.
[3] *The American Economy* (New York: McGraw-Hill Book Company, Inc., 1957), p. 150.

With Professors Knight, Samuelson, and Hansen and other social scientists and educators who have expressed thoughts in a similar vein, we agree that an understanding of economics is important today; that the study of economics should be approached in a thorough, careful, multifaceted fashion; that a grasp of economics can be wedded to visions of a better life. We also feel that informed, insightful, sensitive, creative teachers can introduce, support, and vivify significant aspects of economics in elementary and secondary classrooms.

This volume of the Social Science Seminar Series combines content in economics with appropriate social studies teaching procedures. It has emerged out of the endeavors of two economists and two professional educators. The first six chapters, centered on economics per se, were developed by Professors Richard S. Martin and Reuben G. Miller of the Department of Economics at the University of Massachusetts. Professors Martin and Miller treat the nature of their discipline; the emergence and development of economics as a distinct area of investigation; some questions with which economists are concerned; certain theories, findings, and tools developed and utilized by scholars in this field; and the importance of economics to contemporary man. The last chapter, on classroom methodology, was written by Raymond H. Muessig, Professor of Education at The Ohio State University, and Vincent R. Rogers, Professor of Education at the University of Minnesota. From the preceding chapters, Professors Muessig and Rogers have selected five key generalizations which teachers could explore with children and youth in elementary and secondary schools. A number of methods that teachers might employ to expose students to facets of these fundamental observations have been presented in the concluding chapter. Kenneth E. Boulding, Professor of Economics at The University of Michigan, served as the academic consultant for this book.

The Editors

Table
of
Contents

What Is Economics?   chapter one

> The theory of economics does not furnish a
> body of settled conclusions immediately appli-
> cable to policy. It is a method rather than a
> doctrine, an apparatus of the mind, a tech-
> nique of thinking, which helps its possessor to
> draw correct conclusions.
>
> JOHN MAYNARD KEYNES

"President Asks Congress to Wage War on Poverty," "Longshore
Strike Paralyzes East Coast," "Mayor Submits Record Budget; Taxes to
Rise." Almost every day headlines such as these appear in our newspapers. Economic problems and questions of economic policy are
involved in many news stories and also in many political debates, whether
between presidential candidates or in the halls of Congress. As citizens,
many of us have opinions on these matters and help to make decisions
about them. To choose wisely, we need to be informed about the workings of our economic system and aware of the light which economic
science can throw upon our current problems. A knowledge of at least
some economics is necessary if we are to understand the nature of the
opportunities and problems encountered in the economic life of a society.

At first glance, the economic problems we have referred to may
seem far removed from the events of daily life; yet on closer examination
it is clear that all of us engage in many different kinds of economic
activity. In a widely quoted definition, the British economist, Alfred
Marshall, wrote:

1

> Political economy or economics is a study of mankind in the ordinary
> business of life; it examines that part of individual and social action which
> is most closely connected with the attainment and with the use of the
> material requisites of wellbeing.[1]

Most of us hold some sort of job to earn an income, and most of us spend
money to acquire the goods and services we want. Most people make
deposits and withdrawals at banks and pay taxes. All of these ordinary
activities may properly be called economic behavior. Thus we find ourselves in a position similar to that of the character in Molière's play, who
was delighted to discover that he always spoke in prose. Whether we
realize it or not, economic activity is something in which we all engage.

But in addition to pursuing our separate lives as individuals, we are
also parts of a vast economic system. What we do affects others, and
what other people do affects our own lives and wellbeing. Seemingly
remote problems and actions can wipe out our jobs or increase opportunities for promotion, can make things such as food very expensive or
can provide a wealth of goods at prices most people can afford. Our
material welfare depends as much on the actions of others and the workings of our economic system as it does on our own talents and efforts.
The importance and complexities of the interdependences among individuals will become clear if we look at a few of the distinguishing
characteristics of our modern American economy.

CHARACTERISTICS OF THE AMERICAN ECONOMY

The foundation of economic life in the United States is a vast
network of exchanges or trade. The shrimp fisherman in Florida, the
steelworker in Pittsburgh, and the studio extra in Hollywood are
indirectly tied together and made dependent upon each other by this
network of exchanges. An individual does not as a general rule produce
for himself any significant portion of the goods and services that he
wants and needs. Indeed, he lacks the technical skill required to produce
such things as penicillin, automobiles, television sets, and the host of
other manufactured goods that are part of our standard of living. Any
attempt by an individual to produce such things for himself would be,
if not impossible, at least very inefficient and wasteful. The bulk of the

---

[1] *Principles of Economics* (8th ed.; New York: The Macmillan Company, 1948), p. 1.

goods and services that Americans consume are purchased for money from a large number of private business firms. These organizations, ranging from small individual proprietorships to giant corporations, specialize in various phases of the highly complex task of transforming our society's resources of labor, capital, and natural raw materials into commodities and services.

For a market system such as ours, it is necessary that economic activity be organized in terms of making and spending money. Almost anything—gold, silver, paper, or even cigarettes—can be used for money provided it is generally acceptable to sellers in exchange. It is the functions of money that are important. As the medium of exchange, it serves as generalized purchasing power. Instead of being forced to seek out that person who has just what we want and is willing to barter for what we have, the system of exchange is greatly simplified through the use of money. When we earn money incomes by supplying labor and other services, we are exchanging these resources for the ability to choose a portion of the current output of goods and services.

Economic life is impersonal and highly competitive. We sell to whomever pays the highest price and buy from whomever has the lowest price. The goods produced, sold, and consumed are those for which people are willing to pay a sufficiently high price to cover the costs of resources used in producing them, including profits of business firms. Thus we can say that the central organizational feature of economic life in the United States is the market place toward which all economic activity is directed and through which the activity is controlled.

The features that we have selected lay bare the skeleton of the American economy and show what it is all about. If we wish to go a step further in the process of abstraction and simplification, we can construct a model of the economy which will show the position, articulation, and functions of the parts of the skeleton.

There are a number of ways of constructing a model. The most common type is a three-dimensional miniature representation. A model ship would be an example. Clearly such a model is not possible in the case of an economic system. We are dealing with human behavior, not things. We can, however, use a two-dimensional picture or diagram to illustrate the organization of economic life. This model is similar to the organizational charts that are used to illustrate the functional relations between the various parts of the U.S. Army or of the General Motors Corporation.

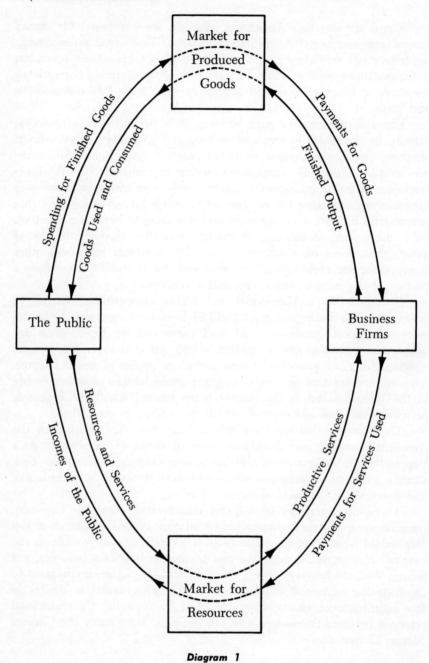

Diagram 1

Diagram 1 provides a sketch of the American economy. The model simply arranges and makes clear the points that were made in our discussion of the main features of our economic life. We see, on the right, that business firms hire productive services and that the payments they make for these services (wages, interest, rent, etc.) become the spendable income of the public. In turn, the individuals and families that comprise the public (on the left in our model) spend their incomes on the goods and services produced by businesses, thereby creating the demands that businesses try to satisfy in their quest for profits.

As the model illustrates, there is a continuous flow of money payments from consumers to businesses and back to the public, matching a flow in the opposite direction of productive services and finished goods and services. It is the counterbalancing flows of money and finished goods and services and productive services illustrated in our model that comprise the myriad exchanges that are the most readily observed feature of economic life in the United States. These exchanges take place in markets that bring together buyers and sellers. In our model we have simplified by categorizing markets according to the general nature of the things traded. It is the entire network of markets in which prices rise and fall in response to the forces of supply and demand that provides the link which binds together the whole set of consumers and producers, each seeking to make the best of his own position and abilities.

The economic system and all that goes on within it is the subject matter of economics. But to define economics, as Marshall did, simply as the science that studies man's activity in making a living is so inclusive as to be misleading. Such a definition implies that economics is the science of things generally, of everything that men are interested in for practical reasons. It tends to make economics indistinguishable from technical subjects such as business administration, home economics, and engineering, which are unquestionably concerned with what can be thought of in a broad sense as the process of making a living. Activities such as production and consumption, buying and selling, are not the exclusive province of the economist. They are part of the totality of human behavior and as such could be studied by the social psychologist who is interested in the development of group habit patterns. Or they could be studied by the sociologist who is interested in the development of economic institutions and their effect on group living. Marshall's definition of economics is so broad that it does not really help us to distinguish this field from other disciplines which are concerned with the same phenomena.

In order to refine our conception of economics, we must know in what respect economists are interested in the process of making a living. The central problem of economics arises from the scarcity of the material means which we have available to satisfy our varied and unending human wants. This problem of the scarcity of material means is a universal fact of human experience. Both as individuals and as a society, we want to have more things and do more things than our means can provide.

When a thing—be it diamonds, money, energy, or even time—is scarce, and there is not enough of it to satisfy all the uses that man would like to make of it, he is forced to choose. It is this act of choice that is defined as economizing. For example, a family may have to choose between a vacation at the beach this summer and trading for a new car. Similarly, a city may have to choose between repaving some bumpy streets and building a new mental health clinic. The peculiarly economic problem associated with the process of making a living emerges as the problem of individual and collective choices in the allocation of scarce resources for the satisfaction of human wants. In order to emphasize this, economists, such as Lionel Robbins, have defined economics as

> . . . the science which studies behavior as the relationship between ends (of various degrees of importance) and scarce means with alternative uses.[2]

In colloquial language, the term "scarcity" is frequently taken to mean insufficiency or poverty; but in the terminology of economics, it refers only to the need for choice in the allocation of material resources. Thus, although it might appear paradoxical, the economic problem confronting man is actually simplified or even eliminated entirely if the immediate problem is one of bare subsistence. When the only problem is that of staying alive, no economizing is required. All that is involved is the purely technical engineering problem of how to produce the most food and shelter with available resources. But man's wants are not limited to physiological needs, and most wants as well as the ability to produce are capable of change and expansion. In our dynamic modern civilization, where we have harnessed the powers of science to control and improve the conditions under which we live, new wants have been generated faster than our ability to satisfy them. The problem of scarcity is thereby perpetuated and even intensified, despite the fact that our wealth and

---

[2] *An Essay on the Nature and Significance of Economic Science* (2d ed., revised and extended; London: The Macmillan Company, 1937), p. 16.

standard of living is far superior to that of any ancient society. If Americans today were content to live at the level of Mexican peasants, all our material wants could be satisfied with but an hour or two of daily labor. We would experience little or no scarcity and economizing would cease to exist as a social preoccupation.

Under the conditions of scarcity, the things that satisfy our wants must be paid for. When we purchase a good it must clearly be paid for with a portion of our money income. However, the real cost of the good is not the dollars spent but doing without the alternative goods and services the money could have purchased. These alternatives include additional leisure time which is paid for by reduced money incomes. The choices which must be made in earning and spending income determine the amounts of resources used as well as the specific goods consumed. Thus, the guiding principle of economic efficiency may be stated either as maximizing the consumer satisfactions from given resources or as minimizing the resource cost of a given level of living.

Recognition of the economic problem as a social problem has occurred only relatively recently. The problem of economizing is virtually as old as man himself, but only in the past two hundred years has there been a systematic ordering of ideas about economic systems and the collection of reasonably accurate data. Early writings on the subject, such as certain passages in the Holy Bible or the Greek tracts on *Oikonomia* (frcm which our word "economics" is derived) were mainly concerned with normative prescriptions. These works set forth the rules for ethically correct economic behavior and specified the "best procedures" for managing a household. Plato and Aristotle, although they treated economic matters, did not distinguish them from political affairs and were mainly concerned with proper organization of the economic life of the state from the point of view of "the good life." In the Middle Ages, Thomas Aquinas wrote of such things as money and wealth from the point of view of the proper code of human conduct that could be logically deduced from the revelations of divine law. It was not until late in the 18th century in the work of Adam Smith that the study of economics was established as an independent subject and science.

The scientific part of economics is distinguished by its abstract character, social point of view, and objectivity. Abstraction is the common characteristic of all science, since the aim of science is to find system and order in the facts and experiences of the real world. The economist is concerned with two kinds of abstractions. First, there is the abstraction of the peculiarly economic aspect from the totality of human behavior.

Second, there are also the underlying regularities that can be used to simplify, systematize, and understand the essential nature of economic behavior and the factors that govern it.

One of the most important abstractions developed by the economist is that of the economic system itself. No one has ever seen the economy of the United States. The existence and nature of the system can only be inferred from the mass of data relating to our economic activity. But the concept of an economic system—the social organization developed to cope with the problem of scarcity—permits the economist to study and relate the economic behavior of each of the individuals and organizations in the system. By viewing our economy as a system, the economist is able to consider all of the factors and forces, direct and indirect, that bear on a particular problem, and to analyze both the immediate and the secondary effects of an action.

In analyzing the workings of our system or the consequences which will follow from some action, the economist makes use of established economic principles or theory. One aim of economics has been the discovery of general principles that govern the behavior of individuals and their interaction within the context of the economic system of society. The body of theoretical generalizations about individual economic activity and the behavior of the economic system that results from it constitutes the core of economics as a formal body of knowledge. Economics, however, is not just theory. The importance of theory is that it serves as an engine of analysis. It guides the identification and collection of economic facts. It permits us to conceptualize and understand new problems and also to recognize old problems that seem always to appear in new guises.

Although economic science is concerned with the general welfare and with analyzing the choices open to us, it cannot tell us what decisions to make. Should we tolerate general unemployment? Should we have socialized medicine? Should we spend tax dollars to support scientific research and development? The answers to these questions depend upon what we believe will be best for our society and the individuals within it. As a science, economics deals with cause and effect relationships, with means to ends, but not with the decision of the goals we should pursue. A broad consensus on the objectives of our society must emerge, as it does, from our political system. While participating in this opinion-forming process, an economist may speak as a responsible professional or as an informed counselor, but not as a scientist. Only after the social value judgments have been made can economic science guide the selection of the most efficient means to the established ends. Thus the main contribution of economics to the search for rational solutions to economic problems is the knowledge it provides of how economic systems operate and why certain causes produce certain effects.

ECONOMIC SYSTEMS: DIVERSITY, SIMILARITY, AND FUNCTIONS

From experience we know that the character and organization of economic life is quite different in different societies. Newspapers and other popular publications report an almost continuous stream of material on the economic life of the Soviet Union and the way in which it compares with the situation in the United States. Information from Great Britain and the Scandinavian countries presents still different alternatives. A study of history indicates that these systems may change dramatically over time. Anthropology supplies us with startling evidence of how great these differences are when we compare the economic system of our modern American society with that of a primitive one. A primary task of economics is to explain both the essential similarities and the nature of the differences in the economic life of different peoples, so that man may be better able to understand the conditions under which he lives and the alternatives that are open to him.

As a contrast to our own economic system, we may examine briefly that of the Zuni Indians of the Southwest during the 1920's. At this time, Zuni society still retained most of its age-old, primitive characteristics. The economic life of the Zunis was that of a self-contained rural community. The chief occupation was farming. Production was carried on by means of simple, easily mastered, traditional techniques and implements that had not undergone any substantial change for many generations. The family was the main organizational unit of their economic life. Each family, comprising as many as twenty-five persons, carried on all of the economic activity necessary to satisfy its own needs. Houses and land were privately owned, with the title being held by the women of the family. Each family worked its own land. There were no wages for labor and no regular production of goods in excess of family needs for "sale" to other members of the tribe. The Zuni ideal was a self-sufficient family within a self-sufficient tribe.

So far, our description of the main features of Zuni economic life seems to indicate that there was no economic system beyond the family.

This, however, was not the case. In important ways, the tribe was an economic as well as a sociological unit. Because of the strongly developed cooperative attitudes and techniques in Zuni economic life, understanding their economic system may prove difficult. In sharp contrast with the American economy, there was a general absence of acquisitiveness and competition. While there was no sale of goods and property at fixed market prices, there was an organized transfer of goods and services that took place within the framework of the tribe. To some extent, these transfers equalized the levels of living among the families of the tribe, preventing the extremes of poverty and great wealth.

The Zuni method of distributing goods among the members of the tribe can, perhaps, be best illustrated by the institution of the work-party. For large tasks—such as planting, harvesting, and house-building—a group of relatives, ceremonial associates, and neighbors were invited to assist the family. Those invited were under no compulsion to attend, and they were not being offered jobs. Some attended for social reasons and others because they were poor. Upon completion of the task, the host's family gave a feast for those who had participated. The size of the feast did not depend upon the amount of work done, but upon the wealth and prestige of the host family. The work-party arrangement was not permanent or reciprocal. The cost of the work-party made it uneconomic for a family to cultivate more land than it needed for its own consumption requirements. This socially-required generosity, plus the fact that the Zuni believed that property was for use, not power, resulted in all wealth in excess of family requirements being freely loaned, bartered, or given away. Stinginess for the Zuni was a greater crime than adultery.

In addition to the work-parties carried on by individuals for their own purposes, the work-party was an important part of the Zuni religious ceremonies to insure tribal well-being. Once a year, in connection with the great harvest ceremony in which the supernatural spirits visited the tribe and blessed it with fertility, a group of the wealthiest families were called upon to finance large work-parties to prepare food for the tribal feast and to build a large house for the ceremony. Through both the family and the ceremonial work-parties, the tribe distributed surplus wealth to its needy members.

The character of the Zuni economic behavior was closely related to their faith in the benign nature of the universe. According to Zuni beliefs, there were supernatural spirits and especially deified ancestors who were concerned with satisfying man's material needs. It was this optimistic fatalism that was the basis for the Zuni's unaggressive, uncompetitive, and generous economic behavior. Power and prestige in this society were associated with non-material privileges, rituals, songs, and war-honors that were never used for economic ends.

It is not possible to do justice to the Zuni economy in a brief account of its main features. As in the case of all small-scale primitive societies, a detailed examination of the entire complex of social behavior is required if we are properly to understand its economic aspects. In this type of society, economic institutions tend to be generalized. The work-party, for example, is economic, but it is held together by a social and political order that transcends the material advantages gained. Our impressionistic treatment of the Zuni economy is, however, sufficient to indicate that the essential organizational factors of Zuni economic life are tradition, custom, and religion.

The critical differences between the Zuni economy and our own should now be clear. As in ancient Greece and medieval Europe, the economic objectives of the Zunis were quite limited. The production of goods and services was carried far enough to insure the survival and stability of the family and the tribe, but the Zuni did not seek to improve levels of living and their control over their environment through use of additional output. Rather than reflecting rational or conscious decisions, what was produced and the methods used were controlled by custom and tradition. Although transfers of goods and services between individuals took place, a system of exchanging goods and services for money did not exist. Yet despite these differences, the primitive Zuni economy constituted a system within which the production and distribution of goods and services occurred in conformity to the values and objectives of the society.

In certain fundamental respects, all economic systems have common elements. All societies of men who make their livings together must inevitably establish and maintain a set of man-made arrangements to supply answers to the basic questions posed by the problem of scarcity. The questions for which every economy must supply answers and in terms of which the system is organized are:

(1) *What commodities shall be produced and in what quantities?* Answering this question involves deciding which of the possible alternative goods and services shall be produced and in what proportions. Food or shelter? Education or entertainment? How much of each? In making these choices, the society must also decide how fully its scarce productive resources are to be used. Less than full utilization means that the problem of scarcity is being made unnecessarily severe. Yet human labor also has

a cost. The devotion of all of society's efforts to the production of goods and services would require the sacrifice of leisure and of the pursuit of man's non-material interests. Some kind of balance must be struck.

√ (2) *How shall the goods be produced?* Some provision must be made for the organization of production and for deciding who will produce the goods, with what resources, and with what kind of technology. Who will farm? Who will build houses? What kind of machinery will be used?

√ (3) *For whom shall the goods be produced?* The total output of consumer goods must be distributed or rationed among the different individuals and families that make up the society. Shall this be done according to their contributions to production or according to their needs? A few rich and many poor? Share and share alike?

In addition to resolving these fundamental economic questions, every economic system must provide the means by which the society may support the activity of its political or governmental authority. Some groups of men must be supported while they perform services for the society as a whole. A system without a tax or levy of some kind is an impossible utopia. But what kinds of taxes shall there be? Property taxes or sales taxes? Taxes which take the same proportion of all incomes, or those which hit the larger incomes harder?

These questions must be and are answered. The vast number of small actions and individual decisions that are required to provide these answers don't "just happen." They are part of a pattern, a system, that is adopted by the society. Whether this adoption is the result of revolutionary change or the by-product of evolutionary growth, whether the decisions reached are deliberate or accidental, each economic system evolves its own answers to these basic questions.

Differences between economic systems depend upon how well and in what ways these questions are answered. Economies may be classified as advanced or underdeveloped depending upon how adequately the problems of scarcity are handled. We can distinguish between economic systems by use of such terms as capitalism, communism, and socialism. This set of "loaded" and generally misunderstood terms refers to the ideological orientation within which economic decisions are made. We may also categorize economies according to the methods used to deal with the problems posed by scarcity: the customs and traditions of primitive societies; the commands issued by a central authority, as in the Soviet Union; the coordination of economic activity via the market system, as in the United States. A variety of different combinations of these characteristics are possible.

Each abstract type of economic system has a philosophy or rationalization associated with it. It is this body of thought that is termed an ideology. Thus the ideology of capitalism attempts to explain why the market form of organization is "good." The arguments contained within an ideology to support a particular ideal type of economy are not limited to the economic sphere. Rather, an ideology justifies the system of economic organization in terms of the general values and objectives of the society. The market economy of the United States is just as often defended because it allows a high degree of freedom as because it has in fact resulted in a high level of living. Men may place different values on different kinds and degrees of freedom. This is clearly a philosophic issue and one on which the battle of the "isms" hinges. When cast in these terms, one cannot prove that one economic system is better than another unless one can prove that certain social values and objectives are better than others. On this point science, economic or otherwise, cannot give us the answer. By contrasting economic systems, we bring into sharp focus the differences in economic organizations and at the same time reveal the differences in men's views and beliefs.

Few, if any, economic systems are pure in the ideological sense. To be understood by the mass of the population of a society, an ideology must be stated in very simple terms. In the process of simplification, distortion inevitably occurs. Most economic systems use a blend of markets, traditions, and commands to organize economic life. An ideology reflects only that organizational principle which dominates. The general acceptance in our society of the values expressed in the ideology of capitalism explains our preference for it. The United States economy is not, however, a pure market economy. The ideology of capitalism as well as the theoretical model of the economy that is associated with it are statements of preference and intent rather than an accurate description of what we really have.

Economic systems and their relationships to social goals and beliefs are not static. Wants and preferences change over time, as do productive techniques and capabilities. The aspirations and values of a society also change, leading to revisions in its economic system. But this process is not a one-way street. Changes in the economic sphere may lead to revisions of society's goals and objectives. It is interesting that one of the methods which may be used to stimulate social change in the underdeveloped economies is the widespread distribution of the Sears & Roebuck catalogue. The knowledge of new possibilities and capabilities may spur drastic changes in both the economic and non-economic aspects of a nation.

An economist is generally concerned with the operation of one particular economy. Once an understanding of the functioning of its parts and processes has been gained, the economist can tell (given the values of the system) how well the system is performing and suggest possible alternatives that would better fulfill the society's goals. With this background, we can now state the common element in the specific economic problems with which we began our discussion. They all involve the failure of the system to fulfill its goals. If as a society we desire full employment of our working population and the economic system does not maintain it, unemployment is an economic problem. Problems exist when reality differs from our mental image of what things should be. In helping to solve these economic problems, the economist contributes to the health and vitality of the social system of which he is a part.

It is a society which organizes its economic activity through the market system that poses an especially interesting challenge to the economist. In the cases of the traditional and command economies, the nature of the organization of economic life and the operation of the systems are easily understood by almost everyone, although the values of these societies might be perplexing to us. In a market economy, however, one is lost without a knowledge of economics. In such a system it is not at all obvious how the questions of what, how, and for whom will be answered in a satisfactory manner by the free interplay of individuals without the guidance of tradition and demand. The economist is thus challenged to explain how the apparently unsystematic system functions. The steps in the historic development of this explanation will be treated in Chapter Two.

Evolution
of Economics
up to 1930

chapter two

> . . . [The early economists were] a handful
> of men with a curious claim to fame. By all the
> rules of schoolboy history books, they were
> nonentities: they commanded no armies, sent
> no men to their deaths, ruled no empires, took
> little part in history-making decisions. A few of
> them achieved renown, but none was ever a
> national hero; a few were roundly abused, but
> none was ever quite a national villain. Yet
> what they did was more decisive for history
> than many acts of statesmen who basked in
> brighter glory, often more profoundly disturb-
> ing than the shuttling of armies back and forth
> across frontiers, more powerful for good and
> bad than the edicts of kings and legislatures.
> It was this: they shaped and swayed men's
> minds.
>
> ROBERT L. HEILBRONER

Everyone knows that the year 1776 saw the propagation of the
American Declaration of Independence. This document was circulated
throughout the American colonies and was widely discussed. In this
discussion, men's beliefs and opinions were changed and clarified. Thus,
the Declaration of Independence contributed in no small way to the
movement which resulted in the formation of a new nation on the Ameri-

15

can continent. But most people do not realize that 1776 was also the year of publication of another work which significantly helped to shape our society. In England there appeared a book with the title of *The Wealth of Nations,* written by the relatively unknown Scottish philosopher Adam Smith. The work was too long and complex to be as widely circulated as the Declaration of Independence. However, through its influence on political leaders, businessmen, and other influential citizens, it too helped to produce a revolution. This revolution resulted in no new nations; but in Great Britain, in the American colonies, and elsewhere in developing nations, it gave birth to a new kind of economic society.

Another consequence of Adam Smith's work was that economics developed as a separate field of study. Gradually men began to specialize in this area, and before many decades had passed, professors of political economy or economics began to appear in British universities. Thus, if any individual must be named, Adam Smith is generally considered the Father of Modern Economics.

What was Adam Smith's contribution, and why did economics develop as a field only so recently? To answer these questions we must look briefly at what had been happening to human society, and to the ways in which men thought about this society.

As Western civilization spread and evolved in Europe, a potential for economic development was created. Villages gave way to towns, and baronies were collected into duchies and kingdoms; combinations of kingdoms produced the modern nation states. By 1750 several rulers claimed the allegiance of millions of subjects, some of whom lived in far distant parts of the world. In the past, when each local area had to be relatively self-sufficient in the struggle against nature for survival, differences had developed both in what was produced and in the methods used. To some extent these differences were dictated by such things as climate and soil fertility. But others were the results simply of historical accident. The cloth produced in each district generally had the same number of threads per square inch, but there were variations in the thread count of cloth produced in different districts. How should these local areas and practices be treated? Was a nation simply a collection of the local societies contained within its geographical boundaries? Some men saw the potential which the increase in communications and trade had produced. The whole could be more than the sum of the parts; if the nation could be welded into an integrated society, the purposes of the state could be better served.

What were these purposes? In general we may say that they were to increase, or at least to maintain, the power and wealth of the state.

In societies just emerging from feudalism, power meant military power; wealth meant the ability to support the military establishment and to provide the luxuries for the courts of royalty and the nobility. Beyond the level sufficient to insure continued supplies of military manpower and goods destined for consumption by the nobility, the economic well-being of the mass population was of no concern. Didn't Christian doctrine teach the value of poverty and humility in this life? Thus, as pointed out in the last chapter, the older conventional or traditional thinking about economic matters combined ethical prescriptions with practical measures to insure political stability and the growth of political power.

During most of the eighteenth century the economic policy and attitudes in Europe, especially in Britain and Spain, reflected the thinking of a group of writers who are called the "mercantilists." Believing that uncoordinated effort would result in confusion and the dissipation of wealth, these men advocated centralized control and policy-making. They thought that colonies could and should be acquired and run so as to strengthen the mother country; that the colonies should be required to furnish raw materials in return for which they would receive finished products. To be successful, colonial trade was to yield a profit in gold to the mother country. The working class of the country should be treated to a large extent as wards of the government; the government should see to it that there were enough, but only enough, workmen in each trade; and, at least in terms of the general level, the wages that were paid should be regulated so as to be "fair." Both the quality of products and the methods used to produce them were to be specified by the government. While it would be a mistake to attempt to draw too close an analogy, a general similarity exists between the approach to economic policy of the mercantilists and that of Soviet Russia today. Both assume that a high degree of centralized control is necessary to promote the economic interests of the state, which is put before that of any individual.

Adam Smith not only denied this assumption of the mercantilists, but argued for its opposite; that the economic well-being of the nation would be most advanced if the government would deliberately refrain from making policy in regard to the products to be produced, the methods of production, the wages of labor, the pattern of trade between colonies and other countries, and a host of related matters. This conclusion followed an entirely different view of economic society. From his moral philosophy Smith drew a new objective for the economic system of the nation. Drawing upon his associations with businessmen and upon what he saw during his extensive travels, he pictured a new kind of economic system. Strangely enough, it was a system in which no person or group of people would consciously make the kinds of decisions that the mercantilists thought the government had to make. Yet these decisions would be made, and most efficiently, by the workings of the economic system itself. *The Wealth of Nations* contained Smith's answer to the hows and whys of the fundamental economic problem.

By the "wealth of nations," Smith did not mean the same thing that the mercantilists had meant. He was not interested in providing the country with the greatest possible military power or with supporting the nobility. Instead, Smith was concerned with raising the level of living of the entire population. At a time when thoughts of political democracy were spreading, Smith voiced a concern for the economic well-being of all members of the society. Since what is consumed must first be produced, he saw quite clearly that the problem was one of increasing the total output per capita. What he called "national wealth" is very close to what we now call the "national income." Thus, in modern terms we would say that Smith was trying to promote the economic development of his country.

If economic development were to occur, labor had to become more productive. But how? It may seem strange to us now, but Smith did not place primary emphasis on the invention and introduction of new machinery. We must remember that Smith was writing at the very beginning of the industrial revolution, and great gains in technology were not yet apparent. For Smith, the most important source of improvement lay in the division of labor. In a famous illustration, Smith discussed the operation of a pin factory. To make a pin required about eighteen distinct operations—from drawing out the wire to inserting the finished product into paper. So many different skills were involved that a single worker trying to do everything by himself might be able to produce only one pin a day. Yet Smith had seen a small factory in which ten specialized men had between them produced about forty-eight thousand pins in a day. Such were the gains from proper specialization and division of labor.

As Smith recognized, the introduction of machinery was only a further application of the basic principle of the division of labor. As a task is broken down into its simpler constituent parts, the possibility of using machinery to advantage is much greater. Gains in agriculture and industry can only be achieved if opportunities for the division and specialization of labor are sought and introduced wherever they are found. Fortunately, we can depend upon individual intitiative on the part of businessmen and farmers to get the job done. Each individual, seeking only his own gain, will be performing this task for society. Since the national income is simply the sum total of the incomes of the individuals within the society, as each person seeks to increase his own income, he is at the same time seeking to increase the income of the whole country. And surely each individual knows far better than someone in a government office where his own best opportunities lie.

But won't the uncoordinated efforts of individuals, each running off in his own chosen direction, simply produce chaos? No, said Smith. The old idea that a nation is simply an expanded family that needs one head or ruler to direct and coordinate the activities of the members is obsolete. In economic matters the "invisible hand" of the market is far more efficient than the material hand of a ruler. What if some particular product is in short supply? Consumers, bidding against each other in the market, will force up its price. New producers will be attracted, like bees to honey, to this trade where high profits can now be earned. The increased demand for the various kinds of materials and types of labor needed to produce the product will force their prices to rise. As labor and other resources flow into this industry in search of higher incomes the output of the product will rise and the market price fall. Thus the competition of individuals, each seeking the highest income for himself, leads to that use of resources which will best satisfy consumers and at the same time make the income of society as large as possible. The economic choices for society are made by the system of markets. If society wants more gloves and fewer shoes, more gloves will be produced.

It was true, of course, that the new system of division and specialization of labor would require the use of more capital. Machinery would still have to be bought. Each manufacturer would have to spend more money to pay his larger work force and to buy the greater quantities of materials that they would use. Producing for large markets instead of to the order of an individual consumer meant carrying inventories of finished products. Unless the capital investment occurred, the potential gains would not be realized.

Here again, Smith relied on individual initiative and the drive to get ahead. The great majority of the rising capitalists, like the thrifty Scotsmen with whom he was familiar, would save a portion of their incomes. Smith approved of accumulation, but not for accumulation's sake. He expected these savings to be put back into business as additional capital. This plowing back of profits is what makes economic development a dynamic process. As incomes rise, saving takes place which automatically increases the quantity of capital. This increase in the quantity of capital in turn makes it possible to support yet more division and specialization of labor. And the increased division and specialization of labor produces yet higher incomes from which still more savings can take place. Thus, once economic development starts, it feeds on itself and continues into the future.

All parts of the society can share in the benefits in this process of economic development. As capitalists save and invest these savings, they will try to hire more labor to expand their output. Wages will rise and even a common laborer will be paid enough to live decently and with minimum comforts. While the ultimate outcome was uncertain, Smith saw no reason why the process of economic development should not be a harmonious one, with the welfare of all classes rising together with the welfare of the nation as a whole.

Smith's urging of a policy of minimal governmental interference in economic matters, which has been given the name of "laissez faire," fell on receptive ears. The governmental controls of the mercantilists had already begun to break down. The rising business classes were increasingly irritated by mercantilistic rules and regulations. Violations of the laws dealing with economic matters were increasing and many of these rules were no longer enforceable. As a result, Smith's policies were rapidly accepted to an astonishing degree. During the recent world wars, we found it necessary to suspend the workings of the market economy and to operate under a system of governmental economic controls. Yet despite the tradition of mercantilist thought, from 1793 to 1815 Britain engaged in the Napoleonic Wars without an extensive system of economic planning and control. Such was the power of Smith's ideas and arguments and the politics of the times.

During the Napoleonic Wars economic events followed a familiar course. The support of Wellington, Nelson, and other military leaders imposed severe burdens on the fledgling economy. Tax increases were not sufficient to finance the war effort and the government engaged in deficit financing with a large increase in the money supply. Inflation followed, but agricultural prices rose more than most. Britain, already an importer of food even in normal crop years, found her foreign supplies cut off. Domestic agriculture was greatly stimulated and agricultural land values and incomes rose rapidly. At the end of the wars, a painful readjustment was in prospect for British agriculture if the market system were allowed to operate unchecked.

To protect their wartime gains, the agricultural interests which dominated parliament obtained a law which imposed a sliding duty on the importation of "cheap" grain. This so-called "corn law" established an import tax or duty which varied with the English price of wheat. Due to the wartime inflation this first law had no practical effect. But in 1813 and 1814 landed interests attempted to obtain a substantial increase in the price at which the restriction on imports would go into effect. A great debate on the corn laws followed, and several disciples of Adam Smith contributed essays or pamphlets to the discussion. The most lasting contribution to economics resulting from this debate was contained in the work of a prominent financier by the name of David Ricardo.

Although lacking in formal education, Ricardo managed at an early age to amass a substantial fortune. Quite by accident he stumbled upon Smith's *Wealth of Nations,* and from that time on, a considerable portion of his efforts was devoted to the study of economic affairs and economic principles. Ricardo had helped to clarify the causes of the wartime inflation and of what had been happening to foreign exchange rates. He was known both as a successful businessman and as a sound and advanced economic thinker.

Ricardo saw the process of economic development as happening in much the way Smith had described it. He was convinced, though, that the corn laws, if kept and strengthened, would bring the process of economic development to a halt. How would this happen? He believed that the corn laws would decrease the incomes of businessmen or capitalists in favor of much larger incomes for the landed gentry. However, the land owners, not being interested in industry and commerce, would not save a portion of their income and add this to the productive capital of the country. In addition, the profit squeeze on the capitalists would keep them from engaging in the expanding world markets for the products of industry. Thus it was important to understand the way in which the amounts of income going to land owners for rent, to labor in wages, and to capitalists as profit were determined. For Ricardo this problem of the distribution of income was the principle one for economics.

If, due to the restrictions of the corn laws, the importation of grains from other countries did not increase as society developed and expanded, the additional food required, as well as the other agricultural products needed, would have to come from British agriculture. This meant that additional land would have to be cultivated, land which was not as productive or fertile as that already in use. To make it worthwhile to use such poor land, agricultural prices would have to rise. This rise in agricultural prices would mean that additional profits would be gained on the older, more fertile farms. These additional profits, however, would not stay with the farmer capitalists who hired labor and actually worked the land; they could and would be siphoned off in the form of increased rents for the landlords. If landlords were to get more, asked Ricardo, who would get less? Not labor, because labor was receiving a wage so close to the subsistence level that no significant decrease in real wages was possible. Caught between the declining productivity of the land, the rising share of the land owners, and the constant real wage of labor, it was the agricultural capitalists whose income or profits would be reduced. But the repercussions did not stop here. As a result of competition among capitalists, the reduced profits in agriculture would lead to a shift of capital from agriculture to other branches of trade, depressing profits in those areas also. As a result of this decrease in profits, capital accumulation would cease, economic development come to a stop, and stagnation set in.

If the corn laws turned the economy onto the road leading to economic stagnation, it was only necessary to repeal them. Free trade would lead to expanded agricultural imports as the population grew and the economy developed. Given cheap supplies of food, the money wages of workers would fall, even though their standard of living did not. With reduced labor costs and with capital permitted to develop the most productive branches of industry freely, a great expansion of output and exports to other countries would occur. These gains would be more than enough to pay for the imported food. Thus, Ricardo's conclusion was really the same as Smith's. Governmental intervention, this time in the form of the corn laws, could only be to the detriment of the economic wealth of the nation.

One of Ricardo's long-time friends was the Reverend Thomas Malthus. At an early age Malthus had published the *Essay on Population* for which he is still remembered. As an outgrowth of his concern with population Malthus produced the theory of rent which Ricardo later refined. Although frequently finding themselves on opposite sides of the fence in economic matters, these two men discussed each other's ideas in a long series of visits and letters.

Besides being the first academic economist, teaching for many years at the college founded by the East India Company to train its young administrators, Malthus was the first English economist to treat the problem of depressions. He was not convinced that in a free-enterprise market economy the process of economic growth would continue smoothly in an uninterrupted fashion. As economic development occurred and more and more goods were produced, wasn't there the possibility of general over-production—a flood of commodities without buyers? Wouldn't saving somehow make the demand for goods too small for the supply? In this area Malthus was never able to develop a convincing formal argument. Ricardo, taking the opposite view—that the economy was always self-adjusting—seemed always to have logical answers to Malthus' points. Despite the hunches which Malthus had, the development of the theory of depressions had to await the overwhelming fact of the great depression of the 1930's.

In one respect Ricardo and Malthus appeared to be in agreement. As Malthus seemed to have established in his essay on population, the long-run economic prospects for mankind were not bright. The gains from economic development might lift the level of living of the masses for a while, but increases in population were sure to follow, leading to pressure on the resources available. When this happened, output per capita would fall, and the mass of the population would be forced back towards the subsistence level. Intervention of the type of the corn laws would, of course, hasten this outcome; but repeal of the corn laws would not eliminate this ultimate prospect.

Writing some decades after Ricardo, John Stuart Mill, the leading British economist of the mid-nineteenth century, came to different conclusions. Following the line of development since Smith, he regarded the laws of production as simple facts which had to be accepted. The gains to be derived from the division and specialization of labor, the most productive ways of combining capital, labor, and other resources, were matters beyond the reach of governmental influence and policy.

The forces governing the distribution of income among laborers, landowners, and capitalists were quite different. As Mill saw it:

> The distribution of wealth, therefore, depends on the laws and customs of society. The rules by which it is determined are what the opinions and feelings of the ruling portion of the community make them, and are very different in different ages and countries; and might be still more different, if mankind so chose.[1]

By this Mill did not mean that there were no economic forces at work to determine the distribution of income. Nor did he mean that society was free to choose any distribution of income it wanted without fear of the economic consequences. He did mean that there was some maneuvering room for public policy in this area. Some readjustments of income were possible without serious effects on the amount of output. Social choices in this area could and should be made.

---

[1] John Stuart Mill, *Principles of Political Economy*, W. J. Ashley (ed.), (London: Longmans, Green & Co., 1909), p. 200.

For Mill economic systems were not fixed or mechanical, but could experience evolutionary change and growth. He accepted the truth in Malthus' proposition that if population rose too fast as economic development occurred, the bulk of the population would always be trapped at the subsistence level. But Mill hoped that another outcome was possible. If the masses could only be given a taste of a better economic life, it would be in their own interest to restrict the size of families. To obtain the initial boost in laboring incomes, Mill advocated giving trade unions a free hand to organize and bargain. This would be clearly an exception to the general rule that society was best served by free competitive markets. Mill felt, however, that this exception was necessary to promote the economic health of the society.

In a sense, Mill represents the end of the line of development which began with Smith. From Smith, Malthus, Ricardo, and others he inherited the reasoning and arguments which justify an economic policy of "laissez faire." By Mill's time this policy had in fact become the policy of the nation. Free trade, both domestic and foreign, was the rule. Interferences by the government were minimal. Yet experience with a "laissez faire" economy led Mill to the conclusion that occasional intelligent intervention by the government in restricted areas was desirable. The legalization of trade unions was just an example. Mill was not able, however, to develop a formal analysis to explain just where and how this governmental intervention should take place. His economic principles were restricted to those of a free private enterprise economy.

In 1848, the same year in which Mill's *Principles of Political Economy* was first published, there appeared also the *Communist Manifesto*. If Mill took a somewhat evolutionary approach to economic reform, Karl Marx's view was a revolutionary one. It should be noted that both men were attempting to do something about the economic conditions of the masses at that time. These conditions were not pretty. The industrial revolution was in full swing. Great Britain, the first country to experience it, could not draw on the assistance of any more-developed country through trade or aid. She had to pull herself up by her own boot straps. Although improvements in conditions of the British working class were being made, the process of growth did not prevent grinding poverty for a significant portion of the population. Readers of Charles Dickens can catch something of the flavor of the times. It was clear that more improvement was necessary.

Mill and Marx reflect the two basic alternatives open to society. Mill advocated the path of reform. Mill, like Smith, rejected total governmental planning and control of economic affairs. The basic system of free and unregulated markets would have to be maintained. But by selected, intelligent intervention, the behavior of both institutions and individuals could be modified to lead to a better world. For Marx, reform was a waste of time. Nothing could be done to change the fundamental character of capitalism. Capitalism may have been a necessary stage in the course of social development, but it was not the end of the road. As capitalism had replaced feudalism, so its own days were numbered. The solution to the problems of capitalism was not *evolution* but *revolution*.

Adapting a concept of the German philosopher Hegel, Marx developed his picture of the rise and fall of social systems. Hegel had been concerned with the process of intellectual development. The advancement of knowledge occurs when two ideas, both partially right, are synthesized into a better idea. Every important statement we can make (which might be called a thesis) is only partially true. The fact that exceptions exist gives rise to its opposite, or antithesis. These two, the thesis and antithesis, are synthesized into a new thesis. For Hegel this was a continuing process with no end. Marx took this intellectual dialectic from Hegel and converted it into dialectical materialism. Marx was convinced that peoples' ideas did not just emerge from the blue sky, but rather were the products of their environment. And since the struggle for earning a living was so important, the economic environment was of primary importance. For Marx history was not a succession of ideas, but rather a succession of economic societies. Each type of economic society, when first introduced, reflected the interests of the dominant economic group. In this way the feudalistic society gave way to the interests of the rising business or capitalist class. But if the new system was in the interest of one class of society, it was not in the best interests of all portions of society. Thus an antithesis would arise, and a new synthesis would be produced via revolution. For Marx capitalism contained within itself the seeds of its own destruction.

Marx saw the fundamental contradiction in capitalism as being the exploitation of labor. He agreed with Smith and Ricardo that all wealth or income was the result of human effort. But the workers who produced the output did not receive it all. Landowners and capitalists obtained their share. How was this possible? Like the other classical economists, Marx believed that the prices of all economic commodities would tend to be equal to their cost of production. Since labor was an economic commodity, this rule would apply to labor also. If a man worked for twelve hours (and the twelve hour day was common), yet could subsist on the output of six hours time, this would be his worth and what he would receive in wages. The balance, after taking into account the wear and tear on capital, was the income of the capitalists and landlords. These two classes lived on the surplus value created by labor, that part of the output of labor which was left after the workers had been paid. This fundamental inequity was the basic law in capitalism. Labor was exploited, although at first it did not recognize this fact.

Marx stated that capitalism would come to an end as the result of a series of worsening depressions. Behaving as Smith said they should, capitalists would save and accumulate more capital. But as they attempted to obtain the larger quantities of labor needed to expand production, they would bid up wage rates. This increase in wage rates would squeeze the profit margins of the capitalists. In an effort to protect their profits they would introduce labor-saving machinery, throwing men out of work. Technological unemployment would produce the reserve army of the unemployed and hold down wage rates. Although the output of goods would continue to increase, the unemployed would not have the income with which to buy these goods. General overproduction would occur and a crisis or depression would follow. The system could survive some crises, but as these grew worse and worse the people would recognize the contradictions inherent in the system. The capitalist class would decline as more and more of this group suffered bankruptcy in crises, the working class would develop a sense of its common interest, and ultimately the system would be overthrown by a revolution.

Marx was more concerned with analyzing the nature and future of capitalism than in describing the Communist state which he expected to follow. As the Soviets discovered after the Russian revolution, his works contained no blueprint for the new society. He did expect, however, that the tremendously productive machine created by capitalism would be combined with a just and equitable distribution of income or output. There would be a classless society in which poverty was eliminated and the exploitation of human beings would cease to exist. Each person would receive what he needed. The government would wither away. Thus Marx was a Utopian or idealist, whose ultimate objectives did not differ substantially from those of the other economists of the time. His primary concern was to raise the level of living of the masses of the population. The difference lay in how this objective was to be reached.

Although Marx belongs to what we might call the underground rather than the mainstream of economic thought, we may include him

in what is called the classical school of economists. From **Adam Smith**
to Mill and Marx there were, of course, technical refinements and elab-
orations of analytical concepts both in Britain and on the Continent
which we have had to ignore. Yet all of these writers had a common
interest, a common view of what economic analysis was, and a common
approach to their problem.

In classical economics the problem was that of the ideal type of
economic system and the role of government within it. Given their view
of man, the classicists were convinced that a free-enterprise economic
system represented an improvement over what had gone before. Since
the market system as a method of social organization was something new
to human history, its essential logic had to be discovered and set forth.
Having chosen this path of economic development, the question of what
lay at the end of the road was a matter of concern.

In line with most late 18th and early 19th century social thought,
these men believed that a relatively few simple economic principles
would suffice to describe the workings of the market system. As Sir
Isaac Newton had reduced the laws of mechanics to a few simple
principles, so they expected to do the same kind of thing for economics.
The economic system itself might be complex but the principles governing it were not. With the qualified exception of Mill, they expected
these principles to be universal in character. Like the laws of physics,
the laws of economics would be applicable to all times, all places, and
all societies.

The method to be used in arriving at these economic principles was
also quite simple. Measurements of economic quantities such as the
national income, or the output, prices, and wage rates in the various
industries, were not available in the mid-nineteenth century. Furthermore, mathematical and statistical methods necessary to analyze this data
did not yet exist. The classical economists were content with creating
simple verbal pictures of the workings of society. By observation of
other people and of the world in which they lived, and by examining
one's own mind and actions, a man could establish the primary facts of
the world and the primary motives which governed man's actions. Once
these primary assumptions and conditions had been established, the
results could be deduced by pure logic. Thus, the economic analysis of
the classical writers was syllogistic.

Between 1870 and 1930 the leading British and American economists
developed what is now called the neo-classical school of economic
thought. Drawing upon the works of the classical economists, these men
produced many improvements and refinements in economic concepts and
analysis. As economics became established in colleges and universities

as a separate and distinct field of study, specialists in this area began to iron out the wrinkles and bridge the gaps that existed in earlier pictures of the economic world. Types of mathematical logic originally developed for application in other fields began to be applied to economics. But the interest in improving economics was not a purely academic one. Marx was acquiring a following among social agitators and reformers, and for political reasons answers had to be found to the Marxian challenge to the free enterprise system. But even without Marx, further developments in economic thought were necessary. The public policy problems of the day required new kinds of economic analysis.

As Mill had begun to recognize, the market system if left completely to itself would not automatically produce the best possible economic world. In a number of industries the competitive market was being replaced by monopolies. Instead of being able to choose among many sellers, consumers were confronted by a single one. In the case of some industries, such as the railroads, monopolies might arise naturally; in other instances competition was destroyed and the companies in an industry were ruthlessly and unnecessarily forced into one unit. In these cases the consuming public suffered from prices which were too high. Where products of poor quality might lead to injuring the health of consumers, even purely competitive markets did not seem to provide adequate safeguards for consumers. Although the exploitation of labor was not a necessary part of the market system, the concentration of power in the hands of a few employers in some areas made this possible. It became apparent that actions which were profitable to the private businessman were not always in the best interest of society as a whole. But if the government were to break out from the corner into which its "laissez-faire" policy confined it, economic analysis would have to be developed to furnish guide lines as to when and where government intervention should take place and what its limits should be.

During this period a few men made major contributions to economics and formulated views that will forever be associated with their names. However, at the same time the profession was expanding and many other men were able to make lesser, but still significant, improvements and refinements in the growing body of economic knowledge. With the growth of professional journals all economists were able to share in the discussions and developments of the subject. Economics had become a recognized field of study with established subdivisions and specialties. Therefore, we must change our approach from that of discussing individuals to one of discussing or treating developments in some of the subject areas in economics.

The first of these areas deals with the question of value, or more explicitly, with the market prices of economic commodities. Since in a free enterprise system markets serve to coordinate economic activity and market prices are important guides to action by buyers and sellers, interest centered on how these prices come about.

The classical economists had distinguished between the ability of goods to satisfy the wants of consumers, which they called the "value in use," and the ability of commodities to command a price in the market, which they termed "value in exchange." Adam Smith had pointed out that water, a most useful and necessary commodity, had practically no economic value; yet diamonds, which were of little practical use, commanded a high price. It seemed that the difference in the market prices of these two goods was due to the difference in the cost of obtaining them. Water was freely available with little or no effort or cost of production and, therefore, commanded a low price. Diamonds were scarce and obtainable only through considerable effort and cost and, therefore, were sold at a high price. For the classical writers, then, cost of production seemed to hold the key to market prices; these costs reflecting the difficulties of obtaining goods from nature.

Yet this view of market prices did not seem quite right. Other writers noted that many things which were scarce had no value at all. Let us imagine that the bakers in a given town produced a thousand loaves of bread to sell on a Monday. Why was it that the bread would sell at just 20¢ a loaf? The key to market price, according to these writers, lay not in the cost of production, but in the explanation of consumer demand. They observed that consumers tended to buy less of a commodity when the price was high and more when it was low. It seemed reasonable to interpret this behavior to mean that when prices were high consumers would restrict their uses of the product to those which were most important to them in terms of the satisfaction yielded. If bread were scarce, very little of it would be fed to the birds. Under these conditions the increase in satisfaction to be gained from buying a little more bread, or to use the more technical term, the "increase in utility" which consumers would obtain from a little more bread would be high. But if consumers are already buying a lot of bread, the increase in utility to be gained from a little more bread would be low. If one thousand loaves of bread will sell for exactly 20¢ each, leaving no bread unsold, and there are no buyers who want to purchase at that price but cannot find bread for sale, it must be because consumers have found a kind of balance between satisfaction and price. They are buying all the loaves of bread which will yield them a greater increase in utility or satisfaction than would spending the 20¢ on other commodities. Any commodity which, although very scarce and difficult to obtain, yields no utility or satisfaction to consumers, will, of course, not be sold at any price. Thus, for these writers, it was the utility of a good which governed its market price.

Neo Classicists

These two conflicting views about market prices were blended by neo-classical economists into a synthesis which included both of them. The English economist Alfred Marshall was a leader in this development. The cost of production in relation to the market price governed the supply of commodities. In the long run only those goods for which the price covered the cost of production would be produced. But consumer demand was also important. What governed price was not supply or demand alone, but the two in combination. For Marshall, supply and demand were like the two blades of a pair of scissors—both blades were necessary to cut anything. But the kinds of interactions between supply and demand were many and complex.

For some commodities, such as the paintings of old masters, for example, the supply is fixed. No cost of production is great enough to increase the number of paintings of Rembrandt or Monet. In these circumstances it is true that the price is governed strictly by changes in demand. If we hold one blade of the scissors fixed, it is the other that appears to do the cutting. Even in this case it is the combination of supply and demand that governs the price. The supply may be fixed, but the level at which it is fixed will have a bearing upon the price.

In the case of goods for which the supply is not fixed, the interaction of supply and demand depends in part upon the time period which we are considering. Suppose that due to a sudden increase in population or a change in consumer taste, the demand for bread in our small town suddenly increases. On the day that this happens, the price of bread will no doubt rise as consumers bid against each other for the thousand loaves that have already been baked. But as soon as bakers recognize that the increase in the price of bread is more than a passing or random movement, they will find that it pays them to increase their output of bread, using more materials and perhaps more labor. As this expanded output of bread reaches the market, the price of bread begins its downward march. If the demand for bread continues at a higher level, bakeries will be earning above normal profits. In the long run additional capital will be attracted to the industry, leading to the opening of new bakeries, or to the expansion of old ones. As this happens, the supply of bread is increased and the price of bread will drop even more. How low it will drop depends ultimately on the cost of production. Thus while at a given time it may seem that either demand or supply has a more important impact upon market price, in reality price depends upon both. It may be more important for us to focus our attention on one more than on the other, but this depends upon the problem that we are interested in or the question that we want to ask.

Some of the implications of this analysis were clear. As a social system the market economy justified itself to the extent that it led to the maximum satisfaction or utility for consumers as a whole. In making choices in markets, consumers would act intelligently only if they were able to judge reasonably well the satisfaction to be gained from various products. Only then could their dollar notes effectively set the objectives for the economic system. At least in the extreme cases in which unde-tectable differences in product quality might injure the health of con-sumers, government intervention was justified. Today we accept the Pure Food and Drug Act as obviously sensible in basic concept. But even this much government intervention into the market system had to be justified. Where monopoly existed, price could remain high and keep profits abnormally high, since the owners of the monopoly were able to control the supply. This meant that an increase in demand would not necessarily lead to an increase in production. The outcome in the example of the bakery industry was the result of competition among bakers. Without this competition production would not necessarily coincide with the wants of consumers. Here again government inter-vention could improve the situation. A natural monopoly such as a railroad could be regulated to control the price charged and the quality of the service. For contrived monopolies or trusts, government interven-tion could lead not to regulation, but to a restoration of competitive conditions. Anti-trust laws could lead to breaking up the Standard Oil monopoly. Thus, this analysis did provide some basis for limited govern-ment interventions in a basically free enterprise system.

A separate question closely connected to that of commodity prices was that of distribution of income. What was it that really governed wage rates? How was the Marxian charge to be answered that a capital-istic economy inevitably involved the exploitation of labor. Several economists, among them the American John Bates Clark, found the answer to this problem. Its logic turned out to be very similar to that involved in the question of commodity prices.

In a competitive economy the price of labor, like the prices of other resources, would be determined by supply and demand. No individual businessman or worker could influence the price in the market. The businessman could simply accept this price and decide for himself how many men to employ. In making this decision he would, of course, be governed by what was profitable for him to do. This profitability depended upon how much each additional man would add to the output of the product. As he increased the number of his employees, he would find that each man would add less and less to the total production. But so long as the additional output could be sold for more than enough to cover the wages paid to him, an increase in profits would result when each additional man was hired. Thus employment would be expanded up to that point at which the output of the last man would sell for barely enough to cover his wages. At this point the last man would be receiving the total value of his output. Since workers could be considered as interchangeable, each man might be considered to be the last man hired. Thus, said Clark, under the market system each worker receives the full value of his contribution to output and no exploitation exists. The Marxian charge of a fundamental inequity in a capitalistic economy was answered.

But in the case of the distribution of income, the advances made by the neo-classical writers had unfortunate repercussions for governmental policy. The theoretical model used by Clark was so convincing that the impression developed that the economy really did operate as he had described it. And if it did, any intervention in labor markets, whether direct (by such devices as minimum wage laws) or indirect (through government sponsorship of collective bargaining), would lead to evil consequences. Any raising of wages above the level set by the market would lead to increased unemployment. At the higher wage levels, businessmen would find it profitable to employ only a reduced number of workers. The wisest public policy, it seemed, was to leave the labor market alone. Marx had been answered, but at the cost of entirely eliminating the possibility that government intervention in the distribution of income would be beneficial. In retrospect, the abandoning of even the limited range of intervention that Mill had visualized was a high price to pay.

If the price and output of an industry are closely tied to the incomes paid to workers and other resource owners by the industry, it is also true that what happens in one industry is likely to affect several others. When the rapidly expanding automobile industry in Detroit offered high wages to attract the additional labor it needed, workers were drawn from many different occupations to fill the assembly plants. Companies in other industries that could not match the higher incomes offered had to reduce their operations or go out of business entirely. Industries and markets are so highly interrelated that the effects of events in one are likely to spread to others, as the ripples spread outward when a stone is thrown into a pond.

This basic truth was reflected in the work of two European economists, Léon Walras and Vilfredo Pareto. The analysis these two men developed is called "general equilibrium theory." In this analysis the important features of an economic system were stated in a set of mathematical equations which reflected the behavior of consumers, businesses, and the system of markets that connected them. Although highly abstract, the work of these men helped to clarify the interrelationships which bound the various industries into one cohesive economic system.

When combined, the work of the neo-classical economists contributed much to our understanding of the way in which a free enterprise economic system functions. So long as consumers are able to choose freely how they will spend their incomes on the goods and services available, market demand will reflect the relative importance of these products in satisfying consumer wants. Businessmen, seeking only their own profits, will be willing and able to attract the resources they need for the production of a good only if consumers value this good more highly than the other things which might be produced with the resources. In this sense the cost to society of producing a product is the goods foregone by having the resource employed here rather than elsewhere. In a pure and free competitive market system, the system itself would lead to the proper allocation of resources and to the proper balances between markets.

Thus if the work of the neo-classical economists laid the foundation for certain types of government intervention, it also raised a warning flag. We would have to be careful to see that the solution to one problem did not create a worse one. Secondary effects and repercussions of any policy, as well as the primary ones, would have to be investigated and analyzed. Considerable knowledge and skill would be required to trace these secondary impacts and to decide how important they were.

Just as the neo-classical economists built upon the foundation laid by the earlier writers, so in the period since 1930 further important contributions have been made to the growing body of economic knowledge. This extension of our knowledge of the functioning of the system and the impact of possible policies has required a much greater degree of specialization within economics. An economist might be a specialist in industrial behavior, money and banking, business cycles, international trade, economic history, or one of several other fields. In each of these areas modern developments reflect attempts to increase the realism or to improve the techniques used to gain an understanding of that aspect of economic behavior. Although starting from the common heritage which we have sketched in this chapter, each specialty has developed knowledge and techniques appropriate to its own field. Chapters Three and Four contain broad summaries of the two major views of economic behavior that have developed to date.

Efficiency and the Economic System

chapter three

As stated in Chapter One, a primary concern in economics is how we may best solve the problem of allocating the resources available so as to maximize the economic welfare of the population. In our treatment of the history of the field, we saw both the development of the free market system as a social mechanism and the evolution of the theoretical structure which enables us to understand how this system solves the problem of allocation. We saw also that certain kinds of government intervention or reforms became necessary or desirable to improve the efficiency of the system. In this chapter we shall survey in broad terms both the efficiency of the American economy today and the major types of public policy questions that are related to the efficiency problem.

It should be noted that the economist attaches a different meaning to the word "efficiency" than does his colleague in the physical or engineering fields. In these other fields the problem of efficiency is simply one of obtaining the maximum output from each unit of resources. For example, an engineer would be concerned with the question of how to obtain the maximum possible energy from various types of fuels. In economics, the efficiency of resource use is defined relative to the wants of consumers. Suppose, for example, that the use of natural gas for home illumination gave the most light per unit of fuel. If so, engineering efficiency would require that homes should be lighted by gas lamps. But consumers dislike the lack of mobility, the odor, the excessive heat, and the unsteadiness of gas lamps. Consumer preference for electric lighting is so great that this is the most economically efficient use of the fuels.

Within limits, the maximum possible economic efficiency is perfectly consistent with some engineering waste or inefficiency.

It is common knowledge that Americans have the highest levels of living in the world. At no other time or place have consumers enjoyed so much of so many different kinds of goods and services. Families in quite modest circumstances now have standards of living higher even than those enjoyed by medieval kings. Part of this economic well-being may be attributed to the abundant resources available to us. Yet the availability of resources is not enough. These same resources were available to the American Indians, but they used these resources so poorly that they were barely able to maintain a subsistence level of living.

Natural resources must be combined with technical know-how to make use of them. Knowing how to use resources is also not enough, however. Knowledge must be translated into action. Unless new products are actually produced and more efficient methods adopted, improvements in knowledge are simply wasted. An efficient economic system is required to exploit the potential open to us.

Although economic efficiency is a key concept in evaluating the performance of an economic system, it is extremely difficult to measure. By examining the many economic statistics collected by government agencies, it is possible to learn in a rough way what allocation of resources has actually occurred. But to judge economic efficiency we also need to know what the alternative allocations of resources might have been and the consumer satisfaction resulting from them. At present we are not able to measure objectively either of these. Although we cannot measure efficiency directly, we are able to obtain some measure of the degree of inefficiency present in an economic system. From information such as the number of unemployed workers, we can gain some notion of the totally wasted productive or economic capacity.

It is also possible to say something about changes in efficiency as time passes. Past experience indicates that our ability to satisfy wants has shown a persistent tendency to increase. Improvements in knowledge have resulted both in expansions in the list of goods and services we can produce and in reductions in the human efforts necessary to obtain them. The expansion in the number of things we know how to do results from the fact that many new goods and services add to our capabilities rather than just replace old ones. New techniques in brain surgery and in psychiatry, while adding to the list of desirable outputs, do not reduce the number of inflamed appendices that have to be removed. Sending a missile to the moon does not reduce the number of commuters who have to be transported to their jobs. These kinds of changes in our ability to satisfy wants have led to the general conclusion that the maintenance of a given level of economic efficiency *requires* that output per person rise over time. Thus it is believed that a complete absence of growth would mean a decreasing degree of economic efficiency in the economic system.

A key concept in this area is the gross national product—the value of all goods and services produced in the national economy during a year. This measure does not involve double counting; it excludes, for example, the output of that flour which is used up by commercial bakeries since this will be included in the value of the baked goods. During 1964 more than six hundred billion dollars worth of goods and services were produced in the United States. This amounted to almost $2750 for every man, woman, and child in the country. This quantity of output was used by consumers for their private enjoyment, by government units for public purposes, and by businesses in the creation of new plants and equipment and in building up business inventories.

To allow us to make better comparisons of the goods and services produced at different times, two adjustments are usually made in the gross national product figures. First, we need to take into account changes in the level of prices. Since prices have tended to increase over the past thirty years, the monetary value of output has risen more rapidly than the actual production of goods and services. Through the use of measures of changes in the level of prices, such as the Consumers' Price Index, the inflationary bias in the figures may be removed. Second, we must consider the increase in the population and the resulting increase in the size of the labor force. By calculating the output of goods and services per capita, or per worker, we can take into account the changes in the size of the population.

Through these and similar calculations we are able to measure a variety of aspects of economic performance. Over the past fifteen years, figures indicate that output per season and output per worker in the economy as a whole have been rising a little under 2% per year. In private industry it is estimated that output per man hour has been rising at about 3% per year. The incomes of consumers have risen fast enough so that on the average each person could purchase almost 2% more goods and services each year. We may conclude that significant increases in consumer satisfaction occurred, even if we do not know what the maximum possible increase would have been.

In the United States private industry has led both in the search for new resources and new knowledge and in the exploitation of such discoveries. Our major domestic manufacturing industries, such as metals, automobiles, chemicals, electrical equipment, and machinery are primarily the result of private initiative and enterprise. The system of free markets allocated added resources to these growing industries, in some cases at the direct expense of obsolete or declining industries. By and large the system worked well.

Yet from the beginning of our history as a nation, the government has taken an active role in the economic system. Protective tariffs were enacted to encourage domestic industry. The Post Office and the military arsenals are early examples of business-type activity on the part of government. Substantial subsidies were paid by federal, state, and local units to encourage the development of railroads. Just over a century ago the land-grant colleges and universities were established with the direct purpose of fostering the growth and improvement of agriculture and industry. While private enterprise was dominant, at no time did the government remove itself entirely from the economic arena.

As economic and social developments occurred, the economic importance of governmental activities increased rapidly. This increase in governmental activity was not the result of a change in ideology or philosophy, but rather reflected what seemed to be the most sensible solutions to the problems encountered. Universal compulsory education was best accomplished by a system of public schools supported by tax dollars. Privately manufactured automobiles and trucks needed a system of public roads and highways. And, as noted earlier, the workings of the free enterprise system itself gave rise to a number of problems which seemed to call for government intervention.

In the complex economic world of today, the problem of economic efficiency is not solved by the market system alone. Government participation and intervention occurs in a large number of areas and in many different ways. This governmental activity may be considered in connection with three fundamental questions. First, which activities should be carried out by the government, and which by private industry. As an example we might consider the peaceful uses of atomic energy. Although the basic research was done by the government, it is apparent that private industry will share in the development of atomic energy. But what is the proper boundary or dividing line in this area? The second question involves such government measures as the pure food and drug acts and the anti-trust laws, which are designed to improve the workings of the free enterprise system. How can we make the private sector of the economy more flexible and efficient? How can we see to it that what is privately profitable is also socially beneficial? The third broad question involves policies to modify the results obtained from the workings of a free enterprise system. Are the results of the operation of the market system fulfilling our social objectives as fully as possible? Since the 1930's we have been gradually exploring Mill's range of choice for public policy in the area of income redistribution through such devices as the progressive income tax, unemployment insurance, and social security. Medicare is a current question in this area.

These three questions are really timeless. Although the broad questions are old ones, the specific problems reflecting them are forever changing. And since today's problems and opportunities did not exist yesterday, the answers of yesterday must be constantly rethought and revised. The efficiency of our economic system depends in large part on the answers to these questions in terms of the problems of today.

In the past, activities were assumed by the government if they were obviously necessary to the well-being of society, and if it was also clear that private enterprise either could not or would not do the job adequately. National defense and the administration of justice have always been considered proper functions of government. Even Adam Smith recognized that certain public works and much of educational activity would have to be accomplished outside of the market system.

Under the general heading of public works, a wide variety of activities developed. In some cases, such as flood control, private enterprise could not do the job. There was simply no way of marketing or selling the benefits of a flood control project in a free market; only through taxation could the necessary funds be obtained. In regard to other activities, such as agricultural experiment stations and reforestation projects, private enterprise simply defaulted. Despite the incentives of the patent laws, the research to improve crop and animal strains and agricultural methods was inadequate. Probably due to the very long period of time needed to obtain a tree crop, cuttings constantly exceeded the amount of new growth. If private enterprise would not do the job, then public enterprise would have to.

The development of atomic energy illustrates how one technological advance can create a whole series of new problems. So much money is involved, and the defense aspects are so important, that fundamental research in this area will no doubt continue to be conducted by the federal government. Yet atomic energy has many peaceful applications as well as military uses. The use of atomic power to generate electricity is one of its most important civilian applications. Several companies are now engaged in building atomic power plants under license from the Atomic Energy Commission. To encourage the development of such plants, the Commission has paid substantial subsidies to companies in this field. But public involvement does not stop with the construction of the atomic generating plants. The privately owned electric utilities using these plants wanted to insure themselves against possible claims for damages in the case of accidents. Private insurance companies, which had been quite willing to provide liability insurance for conventional generating plants, were reluctant to provide insurance for atomic plants. If a nuclear reactor got out of hand, the possible damages were too great and too unpredictable to permit setting appropriate insurance premiums. Government participation seemed necessary to help carry the risks involved in using atomic energy to generate electricity. This led to the question of how much government involvement in a private industry could occur before it became more efficient for the government to assume the entire operation. Yet in many other industries radioactive materials are used without requiring any government involvement beyond that of supplying these materials. Various degrees of involvement are possible and just where the dividing line should be between public and private activity is still obscure.

In recent years economists have found another way in which the concept of efficiency justifies government activity. Suppose we think of a bridge connecting two cities on opposite river banks. Bridges of this type are frequently financed by tolls paid by people who cross the bridge. If the price to cross a bridge is set high enough to pay for the bridge, why shouldn't the bridge be built by private enterprise rather than by the public? Here the concept of economic efficiency tells us that the toll charge must be so low as to be nominal. Prices charged to consumers should reflect the resources used to provide the goods and services involved. But once the bridge has been built, it costs practically nothing in added resources to make use of it. There is, of course, a limit to the traffic the bridge can carry—the maximum number of cars or people that can cross it safely at any one time. Yet up to this limit, an additional person crossing the bridge costs nothing in added resources, and prevents no one else from crossing. Society will be better off if everyone who has even the slightest reason to cross the bridge is free to do so. If some people are discouraged from crossing the bridge because of the toll charge, an opportunity for an increase in consumer welfare with no resource cost is wasted and economic efficiency is unnecessarily reduced. Under these conditions, it has been argued, the activity should be carried on by the government, and be financed from taxes, even if private enterprise were willing and able to do the job.

While certain applications of this principle seem to make sense, other possible applications do not. It is just as true, for example, that within the limits of the seating capacity an additional spectator at a sporting event, movie, or concert involves the use of no more resources than have already been committed. Even in socialist economies, where the reliance on price mechanism is much less, these activities are charged for and are not entirely financed from taxes. Economic analysis can narrow the range of possible choices but does not eliminate them.

While the types of activity in which the government should engage reflect one sort of decision which must be made, the size or extent of each activity assigned to the public sector represents another kind of decision. The volume of goods and services acquired by government for public purposes is not decided by the market system. Instead of the market mechanism, the political mechanism is used to determine the size of governmental budgets. Since the amounts of activities in the public sector and in the private sector are determined in different ways, the possibility exists that these two will not be compatible. In recent years the expenditures of all levels of government have grown so large that renewed interest has been shown in what is called the social balance question: finding the proper balance between public consumption through government and the private consumption of goods and services by families and individuals.

In 1963 more than 120 billion dollars' worth of new goods and services were consumed by all levels of government. This amounted to a little more than one-fifth of our total output of goods and services. By comparison, in 1929 all levels of government consumed a little less than one-twelfth of our total output of goods and services. The greatest part of this increase was due to expenditures connected with national defense. From a relatively insignificant amount in 1929, these expenditures rose to over 55 billion dollars in 1963. In 1963, in other words, some 45% of all goods and services was consumed by government, or almost 9½% of our total amount of goods and services went into the defense effort. Yet this great increase in defense expenditures did not mean that the percentage of our output going into all other governmental activities was reduced. Rather, since 1929 these have increased at all levels—local, state, and federal.

The question of the most desirable balance between the private and public sectors of the economy is even more complex than appears on the surface. To some extent public and private uses of output compete against each other. The more men and other resources we devote to the exploration of space, the less we have available to provide improvements in housing, clothing, food, and other kinds of private consumption. Yet in many cases private expenditures and public expenditures must go hand in hand. New privately owned houses mean new publicly owned water mains and schools. More private cars and trucks mean more public roads and highways. While these connections between public and private activity are quite apparent, there are other links that are less obvious. In a number of cases technological advances achieved for defense purposes have resulted in new or improved consumer products.

Our second major question, that of how governmental activity may improve the workings of the private sector of the economy, may be discussed in terms of three somewhat separate topics. The type and intensity of competition in an industry may be modified by altering the structure of the industry; that is, the number and size of companies in it. In particular market situations it may be necessary or desirable to eliminate or control certain kinds of business practices. A somewhat special case exists in labor markets and involves the encouragement of collective bargaining.

In Chapter Two we saw the need for competitive markets if the free enterprise system were to work efficiently, and noted the passage of the anti-trust laws to allow us to break up artificial monopolies and to restore competitive conditions where necessary. To promote competition and the freedom of opportunity to enter business, we have passed a series of measures designed to protect and encourage small business in general. To some extent small businesses are taxed less heavily than large firms. Within the Department of Commerce, the Small Business Administration provides information and guidance to existing small companies and to people thinking of going into business. It also provides loans if the small business cannot obtain money on reasonable terms from private sources. Efforts have been made to see to it that small firms have an opportunity to share in defense contracts. Laws have been passed to protect small businesses from having to pay too high prices for the things that they buy in comparison to the prices paid by their larger competitors. All of these actions have helped to make industries as competitive as possible, thus increasing the efficiency of the private business sector of the economy.

Yet in a number of our most important industries, it is not possible to have very many competing producers. In these cases the engineering efficiencies of large factories or plants using automated methods of mass production are so great that only a handful of companies can survive. A small automobile assembly plant is simply too inefficient and wasteful to compete with a large one. There is room for only a few companies in the production of electric generating equipment, railroad locomotives, buses, aircraft, and a long list of other products. These markets are not large enough to allow for many efficient producers.

As noted earlier, in the extreme case in which only one firm can serve the market efficiently (which is called a natural monopoly), we developed our system of public utility regulation. To protect the public interest, the decisions of these private businesses in regard to such matters as prices and quality of service were made subject to the review and control of a governmental agency or regulatory commission. If there is more than one, but only a handful of firms serving a market, each firm is subject to some competition from the others, but yet is likely to have substantial market power. In these cases we have not deemed it efficient to apply the public utility type of regulation. Instead, we have attempted to outlaw specific business practices which were contrary to the public interest. Although it is a difficult objective to reach, we have attempted to eliminate false or misleading advertising. To enable consumers to enforce quality standards in what they buy, we have developed systems of grading certain food products, have required food manufacturers to label ingredients on the package, and have required that labels on clothing and certain other textile products show the combinations of fibers used. Abuses of the patent system by companies to increase their market power and profits have been ruled illegal. The relationships between a manufacturing company and its small retail dealers have been examined to uncover and prohibit abuses of market power. In numerous other cases the government has outlawed specific practices which, although profitable to those who engaged in them, worked against achieving economic efficiency, and thus were against the public interest.

In the labor market the generally accepted conclusion was that too often workers attempting to find jobs were confronted by a single employer or only a small handful of employers. The labor market might be competitive on the worker's side, but it was not competitive on the employer's side. By using their market power, employers were able to depress wage rates, to maintain unsafe or otherwise substandard working conditions, and to engage in inequitable treatment. Since it was not feasible to increase the number of employers in many localities, the answer to this problem seemed to be to increase the bargaining power of the workers until it was equal to that of management. To this end we adopted a policy of encouraging and protecting the formation of unions and the development of collective bargaining. As collective bargaining spread and evolved, it became necessary to regulate unions and to prohibit certain collective bargaining practices. In all of these developments, part of our objective has been to increase the efficiency of the economic system.

While attempting to modify the workings of the free market system in the private business sector, we have also found it desirable to modify or adjust the results obtained from that system. In this area, one group of policies pertains to the distribution of income. Our income tax system takes a higher percentage of large incomes than of small ones, leaving incomes after the tax more equal than they were before. Through the minimum wage laws, the social security system, unemployment insurance, and similar devices, we attempt to provide a minimum or floor to the incomes of our citizens. But as Mill recognized, in a free enterprise economy there are limits beyond which we cannot push in equalizing incomes without suffering economic penalties. In a market system differences in incomes provide the incentives to spur private enterprise and to get labor and other resources to move to those uses which will maximize economic efficiency. In the tax cut of 1964, discussed more fully in the next chapter, the rates on large incomes were cut more than those on smaller ones. The purpose of this was not so much to promote the interest of that minority group with above average incomes as it was to promote the general welfare. The conclusion had been reached that the high tax rates had so weakened economic incentives that growth and development were being inhibited. One of the limits had been passed.

A second type of problem involves particular industries in which, for one reason or another, the market system fails to bring about an efficient allocation of resources. An outstanding example of this problem can be found in American agriculture. During the interwar period, agriculture appeared to be chronically depressed. Supplies of farm products exceeded the demand for them at prices that would cover costs. Most farmers did not share in the general prosperity of the 1920's. In the Great Depression of the 1930's the bottom fell out of agricultural markets. Prolonged hard times resulted in considerable suffering and unrest among farmers. The market system, left to itself, seemed to be incapable of bringing about a proper balance between the resources used in agricultural production and consumer wants. The first major intervention in agricultural markets occurred under the Hoover administration. Other drastic programs were adopted during the New Deal.

Part of what we commonly call "the farm problem" involves economic underdevelopment. Some sections of the country have not participated in the growth of modern industry and commercial agriculture. Using obsolete methods on small and poor plots of land, families farming in these areas are still close to the subsistence level. But this is only part of the problem. Without government intervention many agricultural prices are subject to rapid and wide fluctuations. Boom years may be quickly followed by bust years. During hard times even progressive, efficient farmers may be unable to avoid bankruptcy. Still, very few farmers can afford to abandon their homes and land and seek employment elsewhere. Thus hardship and suffering does not result in the socially desirable movement of excess resources out of agriculture, leaving only the most efficient producers in this field.

Through government programs we have provided temporary relief from the instabilities of agricultural markets and have stabilized agricultural incomes. But it must be recognized that we have not yet solved the economic problem of over-capacity in agriculture. Both crop surpluses and the inefficient use of agricultural resources persist. In recent years the productivity of farms has been rising even faster than that of manufacturing industry as a whole. Despite our growing population, the number of farmers required to produce our crops and livestock is still declining rapidly. While people have been leaving agriculture, we have not yet found politically acceptable methods of speeding this process to the point consistent with economic efficiency.

In some cases, as in agriculture, a depressed or declining industry can affect a whole region. The declining use of coal since World War II has made most of the Appalachian coal field a distressed area. Here again it became apparent that the market system was not producing a reallocation of these resources. Men and other resources were simply idle and their potential contribution to the output of society was wasted. Similar problems exist in the case of certain industries which have suffered from competing imports because of the changing pattern of international trade. The expansion of international markets may hold considerable potential benefits for society, but these can be realized only if the displaced resources can be usefully employed in other industries.

The problems of guiding the redevelopment of distressed areas and the reallocation of resources from distressed industries are so difficult in our complex economy that we have only begun to settle them. Since 1960 programs have been adopted to aid distressed areas and to help in the readjustment to changing patterns of international trade. Yet these programs are only a beginning. Much needs to be learned and many experimental programs need to be developed to enable us to discover how to assist our free enterprise system in achieving an efficient allocation of resources without impeding or destroying the system itself.

In another series of developments since World War II we have attempted to stimulate the research and development of new products and improved methods. Both for defense purposes and to increase the rate of economic growth in general, we have changed our approach to the advancement of knowledge and new inventions. No longer do we regard new inventions or discoveries as simply the result of the birth of peculiar geniuses. Instead, we now treat technological advance as one of the things we can produce, as one of the outputs of our economic system. Through the tax laws the government has encouraged the research and development activities in private industry. But in addition, we are now spending several billions of tax dollars each year to support research and development projects. Aside from defense projects, the National Science Foundation and some other governmental agencies devote most or a substantial part of their budgets to these activities. By government intervention in this area we hope to speed the process of economic development and thus to improve the welfare of society as a whole.

In this chapter we have been concerned with the problem of how best to allocate our scarce resources so as to satisfy the wants of consumers. How well this problem is resolved in relation to the possibilities that exist at some point in time is termed the economic efficiency of our system. Since the United States enjoys one of the highest standards of living in the world, it is fair to say that we have a relatively high degree of economic efficiency. In both the past and the present our system has relied primarily on private enterprise and initiative, subject to the competitive restraints of market forces, to allocate the bulk of our resources. But there has also been a rising trend in the role of government. There has been an increase in the exercise of the government's power to provide goods and services for public use and to intervene in the operation of the private sector of the economy. These activities have been undertaken in the pursuit of economic and non-economic values and objectives.

Although answers have been found to some of the public policy problems discussed, solutions to others are still being sought. After looking at the performance of the economy as a whole in Chapter Four, we shall then turn to the current research in economics from which additional answers may be derived.

The Performance
of the Economy   chapter four
as a Whole

Our system is depressive-manic;
It runs to boom, or else to panic.
In view of this it would be wise
For Government to Stabilize—
Remembering the need for both
Stability and steady growth,
And that inflation dulls the enjoyment
Even of constant full employment.

KENNETH BOULDING

On February 26, 1964, President Johnson signed into law what is known officially as the Revenue Act of 1964. This act sharply reduced the income tax rates paid by individuals and corporations. Reductions in taxes are always welcomed by taxpayers, but the purpose of this tax cut was not to ease the burden on the tax-paying public. Rather, the act was one of a continuing series of adjustments made by the federal government to control the over-all level of economic activity in our country. By the level of economic activity we mean the rate of production of goods and services, the level of employment in our work force, and the amount of income earned in the production of our output. These three things are so closely related that we may speak of any one of them as a measure of the level of economic activity. Despite its age, economic science has only in relatively recent times been used to study intensively the determinants of the level of economic activity and to

47

suggest the means by which this level may be controlled. It is just in the last thirty years that our government has accepted responsibility for controlling the level of economic activity. In this chapter we shall see how the need for governmental policies of this type evolved and how the level of economic activity may be influenced. The tax cut of 1964 may be thought of as a recent and well-publicized example of this branch of economic analysis and of public policy at work.

Major changes in taxes are not undertaken casually or frequently. The tax cut of 1964 was the first large peacetime change in the income taxes paid by individuals and corporations in a decade. Earlier tax reductions in 1948 and 1954 had been part of the return to "normalcy" after the more or less temporary tax increases during World War II and the Korean Conflict. According to the estimates of the U.S. Treasury Department, the Revenue Act of 1964 should have resulted in at least a six billion dollar reduction in tax payments by individuals in 1964 and a further three billion dollar reduction in 1965. In addition, tax payments by corporations would be reduced by an estimated two and one-half billion dollars during the period 1964–65. The magnitude of these reductions is considerably larger than those that resulted from the tax cuts in 1948 and 1954; and the motives for the 1964 action were quite different.

When President Kennedy first proposed the tax cut in early 1963, economists and politicians were uneasy about the existing state of the economy and what the future would hold. Judging from conditions in the month of February, when the unusually large number of five million workers (nearly 7% of the labor force) was unemployed, it looked as though another recession was imminent. No one could be certain because the month of February is usually a month of relatively high unemployment; but if the pattern of activity suggested by the high February figure were to continue, unemployment in 1963 would be equal to or greater than that experienced in the recession of 1961. Thus, when first proposed, it was generally thought that the main purpose of the tax cuts would be to stimulate economic activity and thus prevent a recession.

Congress was very slow in reacting to the President's proposal. As the months went by, it became clear that a cyclical slump was not developing. Unemployment did not rise but neither did it fall. In these circumstances, little justification could be given for tax cuts as a means for preventing a recession. However, the President's proposal was not withdrawn. Instead, the main emphasis in argument for the action was shifted from the problem of economic instability and unemployment to the closely related problem of economic growth and development. Thus it was claimed that tax cuts should be used to speed up the rate of economic growth and "get America moving again."

Since 1957, the Gross National Product had not increased according to expectations. Recessions, although mild, seemed to be coming more frequently and recovery was not as fast or as vigorous as in the past. Unemployment during the period had averaged 6% and had not fallen below 5% of the labor force. Many industries had idle plant capacity. Although output was rising, we were not producing as much as the labor force and other resources would permit. Potential output was being wasted. Even though the economy was not really in a recession, it was estimated that at the end of 1963 we were producing goods and services at a rate of about 30 billion dollars short of our potential full employment level.

Thus, although 1964 was a presidential election year, the purpose of the tax cut was more economic than political. Presumably most voters favor tax reductions as long as these reductions do not have unfortunate consequences. We expect the federal government to manage its fiscal affairs responsibly; yet at the time the tax cut was proposed, annual expenditures were running ahead of receipts and the federal budget showed a deficit of 12 billion dollars. In this situation were reductions in tax rates responsible or irresponsible? The proposal generated a flood of arguments and counterarguments, both in Congress and in the press. The tax cut debate focused nationwide attention on, the question of the society's goals with respect to economic stability and growth and the proper means of achieving them.

Recessions and inadequate rates of growth both represent serious deviations from society's goals in that both conditions result in unnecessary unemployment and waste. In a free enterprise economic system, some unemployment is inevitable. When young people leave school and enter the labor force for the first time, there is generally a short wait before they start their new jobs. There are always workers who have just quit their last jobs and have not yet found new ones. It takes time for workers laid off in one industry to find employment in others. These types of unemployment will always exist in a free economy, even if there are more than enough jobs to go around. For this reason, the goal of full employment does not mean that no person is unemployed, but rather that the unemployment which exists is of this temporary or, as it is called, "frictional" type. While the amount of this frictional unemployment varies from time to time, it is considered by the Council of Economic Advisers and others to involve generally about 4% of the labor force. Recessions and inadequate growth lift the level of unemployment above this minimum. Levels of unemployment significantly above this 4% figure mean that many workers who are willing and able to work are unable to find jobs. If this situation persists for any length of time, it means considerable hardship and suffering for the families and individuals involved.

But the personal hardships of these individuals are not the only cost to society. When unemployment is high, labor and other resources are being wasted. So long as we have not run out of worthwhile uses of additional output (and it seems unlikely that we shall face this situation within the foreseeable future), some increases in the production of goods and services are always desirable. The goal of full employment is directly connected to the goal of obtaining the maximum useful output of goods and services now and obtaining sustained economic growth for the future.

If high levels of economic activity and high rates of growth are desirable in terms of the additional output which results from them, they contribute also to the resolution of a number of other problems, both economic and non-economic. On the international scene, economic strength enables us to support foreign aid and defense programs without unduly restricting the consumption of goods and services by our civilian population. In the battle of ideologies, a good record of economic performance adds to the prestige of the free world. We should recognize also that a healthy international economy requires a high level of activity in this country. Because so many countries sell commodities to us, their levels of output and employment are tied to our own. A recession here is likely to be exported to other nations, leading to the latter having greater unemployment and reduced incomes. Within our own country, full employment aids the reallocation of resources from declining industries and areas. To move labor and other resources out of farming requires that there be opportunity for useful employment elsewhere. It may even help to relieve racial problems. It has been observed that during periods of full employment, less discrimination in hiring and promotion occurs, since the alternative to employing a Negro or a member of some other minority group is likely to be having no one to do the job. Individuals from minority groups are often the last ones hired and the first ones laid off.

As the debate on the tax cut developed in 1963, it became clear that a majority of economists did not oppose some sort of tax reduction. Since 1946 there has been within the executive branch of the government an organization known as the Council of Economic Advisers. This three-man council and its staff have the responsibility of keeping abreast of changes in our economy and of recommending to the President whatever programs are necessary to promote full employment and production within the framework of free enterprise. The council played a major role in developing the proposal submitted to Congress. Within Congress itself, an important part is played by the Joint Economic Committee. Established by the same law which created the Council of Economic Advisers, the Joint Economic Committee includes members of both the House of Representatives and the Senate. This committee holds public hearings on the annual economic reports of the President and on laws involving important economic changes. During these hearings, the views of both governmental and private economists are obtained. In the course of the hearings on the tax bill, it became apparent that, while there might be differences of opinion as to the proper size of the tax cut, the timing of the cut, and the particular taxes or tax rates which should be cut, there was general agreement that some action in this direction was feasible.

The economic reasoning used in the analysis and discussion of the tax reduction proposal of 1964 was very different from that which would have been applied in earlier times. As we saw in Chapter Two, the classical economists expected the system of markets to achieve the appropriate level of activity for the system as a whole, as well as in the market for each product or service. In his debates with Malthus, Ricardo always took the position that the economy was self-adjusting. If demand grew more rapidly than the production of goods and services, the increase in the general level of prices surely would choke off the excess demand for resources and return the system to the proper level of activity. If general unemployment occurred, it meant only that the price of labor was too high. Competition among the unemployed would lead to reductions in wage rates and this would make it profitable for employers to hire more labor. The problem would be solved. With freely moving prices for products and resources, the market mechanism would always tend automatically to remedy any undesirable conditions.

Starting with Adam Smith, these views dominated economic thought and policy for more than a century and a half. Occasional doubters like Malthus were not able to challenge successfully the accepted picture. Governments adopted the classical theory and followed policies of nonintervention in determining the level of economic activity. Recessions and depressions occurred, but sooner or later these were followed by recoveries and expansions without governmental assistance. Although it appeared to some that the ups and downs of the cycle were becoming more severe, the best policy seemed to be to allow the market system to right itself. The great depression of the 1930's changed all of this.

Although danger signals had been developing for some time, it was the stock market crash of October 1929 which made most people realize that trouble was ahead. There were, to be sure, temporary interruptions in the trend, but for more than three years the pace of economic activity continued to fall. The bottom was not reached until the winter of 1932-1933, when some fourteen million people, or more than one-quarter of the total labor force, were completely unemployed. Many others had only part-time work. During the three-year decline, the output of goods and services fell about 30%. Due to the drop in prices, the market value of this output was only about half that of 1929. More than eighty-five thousand businesses became bankrupt and some nine million savings accounts were wiped out. The life savings of countless individuals suddenly disappeared. It looked as though the country were coming apart at the seams.

Clearly, something had to be done—not just to alleviate the suffering, but to correct the economic situation. It might still be true that, left to itself, the market system would sooner or later bring about a recovery and return the economy to full employment. But even if this were so, the cost would be too high. The policy of non-intervention by the federal government would have to be changed. What policy should be substituted for it? Intervention might take many forms.

Some took the position that the entire system of free markets would have to be drastically altered. These people looked to government planning to put the idle resources to work again to produce the goods and services so desperately needed. If the market system could achieve only such a poor utilization of resources, surely government intervention, planning, and controls could do better. The records of Hitler's Germany and of the Soviet Union in avoiding serious general and involuntary unemployment showed that there was some truth in this position.

To most people, the solution of doing away with the free market system entirely was too drastic. Even if total government planning were possible, and many doubted that it was, this solution to the problem of unemployment would carry other high costs. Economic efficiency and individual freedom would both surely suffer. Instead of scrapping the market system entirely, some means would have to be found to enable limited types of government intervention to keep the economy close to the goal of full employment.

The rough outlines of how this could be done were pointed out by the brilliant British economist, John Maynard Keynes (who later became Lord Keynes). In a hastily written book published in 1936 with the awesome title, *The General Theory of Employment, Interest, and Money,* he described a new approach to the problem of maintaining full employment. This book contains some errors and is by no means a finished work. Corrections, improvements, and additions have been made by other economists since 1936. Still, the essentials of Keynes' analysis underlie our present understanding of what determines the level of economic activity and current governmental policy in this area.

‸ According to Keynes, the picture of a free market economy always tending automatically toward full employment did not correspond to the real world in at least one respect. The key difficulty involved the classical assumption concerning the flexibility of money wage rates. As we noted above, the classical economists expected that general unemployment would be corrected through a fall in wage rates that would make it profitable for employers to hire more workers. In order for this to happen, however, the prices of goods and services sold by business would have to stay the same or fall by less than wages. From the workers' point of view, a reduction in wage rates not matched by an equal reduction in prices would mean a cut in real wages, *i.e.,* the amount of goods and services they receive for their labor. As Keynes pointed out, the problem was not so much that the workers refused to take a cut in their level of living during a depression, but that employees and their union leaders seemed to think that changes in money wages were important, regardless of what happened to prices. Thus money wages simply were not very flexible in a downward direction. After winning a raise from employers through hard individual bargaining or union negotiations in good times, to give it up during a recession appeared to be a retreat and an admission of defeat. The resulting "stickiness" of money wages meant that wages could not be reduced quickly and easily to the level required for full employment.

It might appear that the logical thing for the government to do would be to force wage rates down to the level which would bring about full employment. Keynes said no. Not only was this course of action politically impossible, it was also unnecessary and undesirable. Events in labor markets were the results, not the causes, of recessions and depressions. The primary causes of economic instability lay elsewhere. In his hunch that the level of saving was somehow connected with recessions and depressions, Malthus had been correct. What Keynes did was to show what these connections were and to build up analytical tools for dealing with them.

To gain an understanding of the Keynesian analysis, we must start from the picture of the circular flow of economic activity described in Chapter One. In this picture, all productive activity takes place in what we call the business sector. One result of this activity is the output of all newly produced goods and services sold to the public. The value of this output is, of course, the gross national product. In producing this output, businesses make use of the labor, capital, and other resources that are supplied by the public. All income paid by businesses to the owners of these resources stems from the receipts gained in selling the gross national product.

What we call "the public" in this view of the economy contains more different elements than is apparent at first glance. Households which supply labor and other resources and purchase part of the current output for their private purposes are, of course, included. Governments, to the extent that their activities involve taxing consumers and businesses and purchasing part of our national output for public purposes, are also placed here. This sector contains, in addition, the activities of businesses in the purchase of new plants and equipment. Part of our national output consists of these additions to our productive capacity. Since these items involve sales from one business to another, a complete list of the purchasers of our current output of the business section must include business itself. Thus, investment activities of businesses are also shown in the public sector.

The level of activity in the productive or business sector of the economy, which determines the amounts of labor employed, of other resources used and of incomes earned, is directly influenced by the actions of the public. The resources supplied by the public limit the amount of production which can take place. But since what is produced must be sold, the level of productive activity is also limited by what the public will purchase. Full employment of labor and other resources, then, requires that the public be ready, willing, and able to buy that quantity of goods and services which can be produced from these resources.

 ˙˙ Keynes found the key to recessions and depressions in the behavior of the public sector. A reduction in the level of economic activity means that there is unemployment of labor and other resources. The trouble, however, does not lie with the supply of resources. Jobs are wanted by as many workers as before; they simply cannot find them. The difficulty is that businesses cannot sell all their output. The total demand for goods and services is too small.

To understand why the total demand *can* be too small, we must look at the savings and investment activities of the public. By savings we mean that portion of current income which is not spent to purchase goods and services for consumption. Investment means the purchase of plant and equipment to expand or improve our productive capacity. From the time of Adam Smith, it was recognized that savings and investment were connected. When people save, this means that not all resources will be required to produce consumer goods so that some resources are freed for the production of capital goods. Savings also provide the money which capitalists can use to finance the purchase of new plants and equipment. Thus, it may appear that what is not spent on consumption will automatically be invested. But this will only be true if savings equal investment.

Keynes pointed out that in our modern economic system the decisions to save and invest are made by different groups. The great bulk of the saving is done by households or consumers. Investment decisions are made by business men. Since these interdependent decisions are made by different people, the total amounts these different groups would like to save and to invest will not necessarily be equal.

The implications of differences between the amounts of planned savings and planned investment may be seen if we examine what has been called the "paradox of thrift." Suppose that at some time the public decided to save the entire amount of its income. If the total amount of income is to be saved, nothing can be spent to purchase newly produced goods and services. If there is no demand for goods and services, nothing will be produced. If nothing is produced, there will be no employment and also no income. Thus, an attempt to save the entire amount of incomes would be self defeating; there would be no incomes to save. Smaller differences between planned investment and planned savings will have less serious impacts on the level of economic activity, but the extreme case may help to make the principle clear. If planned investment exceeds planned savings, the levels of total demand of the economic activity will rise; if the reverse is true, total demand for production will fall.

This analysis by Keynes carried with it a rather unsettling implication. If planned investment just equalled planned savings, the level of total demand would remain constant. There seemed to be no reason to think that this equality between the two would occur only at a full employment level of activity. It could happen when substantial unemployment existed. If it did, the economic system would have no tendency to return toward full employment. Instead of always heading toward full employment, the economy was more like an elevator: while it could move up and down, it could also stop and remain at any level, depending upon the propensities of the public to save and to invest. Continuous intelligent management by the government was therefore required to move us toward, or keep us at, a full employment level of economic activity.

As the "watchdog" of the level of economic activity, the Council of Economic Advisors constantly makes estimates of trends in the level of total demand. Research indicates that regardless of the behavior of individuals, consumers as a group behave in a fairly predictable fashion. They spend most of their current incomes for new goods and services, but they also have substantial savings. Furthermore, as the level of their incomes changes, the amounts spent and saved vary in a fairly regular way. As consumer incomes rise, a portion of the increase will be used to expand consumption expenditures, while another small part is added to savings. While the level of incomes is not the only factor determining the amounts consumers will spend for new goods and services, it is clearly the most important one. This relationship was observed by Keynes and has been given the name of "the consumption function."

If the demand for goods and services by consumers is fairly predictable, that of business units is not. Purchases of new goods and services by businesses are in the forms of new construction, new equipment, and additions to stockpiles of goods or inventories. These investment expenditures by businesses are not, in the main, geared to the current level of business activity and incomes. They involve building for the future rather than for the present. For a business to build a new plant, it must be convinced that the expenditure will result in profitable future operations. Thus, expectations about the future are of critical importance in deciding how much investment to undertake. Since the level of investment expenditures is so important and yet so changeable, periodic surveys of business trends are conducted to find out what the expectations and plans of business are for the future.

In this simplified view of the economic system, the government also plays a role, and one which is fairly complex. Governments also acquire newly produced goods and services for public purposes. In so doing, they add to the total demand for new output. But governments also tax business and consumers to obtain the revenues they need. These taxes give governmental units control over a share of the incomes earned by businesses and households. If tax receipts are larger than governmental expenditures, a surplus of receipts occurs. When this happens, the government is acting like consumers, and not spending all of its current receipts. An excess of expenditures over the tax receipts creates a deficit. When this occurs, government, like business in its investment expenditures, is spending more than it can finance from current income.

Thus governments add at some times to consumer savings and at other times to total investment.

Although many kinds of government activities are relatively stable or grow quite smoothly, others behave in an erratic fashion and increase the instability of the economic system. Education and highway construction are examples of fairly steady programs. The most clear example of the opposite type of program is the defense effort. Each war or police action means a big upsurge in defense spending, followed by a subsequent reduction. But even without a "hot" war, we have been devoting 10% of our total output to defense activities in recent years. Whether defense spending will rise or fall clearly depends upon the international situation. Since these expenses are now so large, any significant increase or decrease in them will be felt by the economic system.

Short-term changes in the level of economic activity, such as recessions and their recoveries, depend upon the interplay of all of these forces. Consumers, businesses, and governments all make up part of the total demand for new goods and services. As we have seen, some of the parts of this total demand are fairly stable and predictable. Others, primarily business investment and national defense spending, are quite unstable. The instability of the latter means that the total demand for goods and services, and with it the level of economic activity, is likely to fluctuate unless deliberate efforts are undertaken to stabilize it.

When we shift our focus from these short-term fluctuations in the level of economic activity to the long-term process of economic growth, the nature of the problem and our analysis becomes much more complex. Everything we have said about the importance of total demand is still relevant, but now we must also consider total supply and the various factors that influence it. The goal of continuous growth with full employment involves a delicate balance between increases in the society's productive capacity and the amounts of new goods and services for which consumers, businesses, and government are willing and able to pay. The actual growth in output over time will be determined by the growth of demand and supply, according to which is the smaller and hence the limiting factor. Not only must these two elements in the growth process be maintained at a high level—they must also be kept in balance. Undesirable results in the form of chronic, long-run tendencies toward inflation or unemployment may be expected from a lack of balance between the rates of expansion of total supply and demand.

On the supply side of the economy, growth requires that we constantly increase the quantity and productivity of our resources. A growing population adds new workers to the labor force. But to employ these new workers efficiently, there must be new investment in capital goods for them to work with. Increased amounts of natural resources are also required to produce greater output. Economic growth, however, is not dependent solely or even mainly on a greater quantity of resources. Growth and development usually mean doing new things or doing old things in new ways. To produce more output per worker, we must have the technological knowledge that tells us how to do it. More training is required and new skills may have to be developed in the labor force. The market system must see to it that the money needed to finance the expansion and the other resources required are made available to the proper industries. As described in the last chapter, the appropriate social balance between governmental activity and private production must be achieved. In general, the market mechanisms and the relevant public policies must see to it that the level of economic efficiency in our system is at least maintained and perhaps improved. All of these requirements must be met if growth is to occur.

Economic growth provides a special challenge to our society because many of the qualitative changes that we have indicated are required to make growth possible. These changes are only partially economic in character. Technology, for example, depends ultimately upon the quality of our scientific research. The flexibility and initiative of the work force is heavily conditioned by social customs and attitudes. Economic costs are not the only ones incurred in the process of economic growth.

, In attempting to control the level of activity in our economy and to realize society's goals with respect to growth and stability, there are several tools which the government may use. Some of these, which constitute what is called "monetary policy," are concerned with adjustments in the cost and availability of money and credit. The workings of our monetary and banking system and of financial markets are so complex and contain so many technicalities that we have had to ignore them in this introductory overview. For the present, it is enough to know that the federal government, through the Treasury and the Federal Reserve System, is in a position to control the total amount of money in circulation and to influence interest rates. Through its regulations affecting the banks throughout the country, the government is able to limit the amounts which can be lent to businesses and other borrowers. By these and other means, the government has an influence on the total supply of financial capital which is available to finance new business investment.

When they undertake major expansion projects, businesses usually have to obtain some of the funds required from outside lenders or investors. Part of the new plant and equipment may be paid for from profits which are plowed back into the business, but frequently these profits are not large enough to do the whole job. Under these conditions, the ability of the business to carry out the expansion project depends upon its ability to locate new investment funds; and since the new money obtained must be paid for, even the desirability of expansion projects depends in part upon the cost of these funds. If money and credit are expensive and difficult to obtain, the ability of business to finance new expansion projects will be restricted. If, on the other hand, money and credit are cheap and readily available, investment expenditures by business will be encouraged. Thus, through its controls over the supply of money and credit, the government is able to restrict the investment expenditures of business or to encourage an expansion of them.

Unfortunately, monetary policy is not as effective in stimulating an increase in the level of economic activity as it is in restricting excessive business investment. If businesses plan too high a level of investment expenditures, monetary policy can prevent some of these plans from being put into effect by making it difficult or impossible to obtain the funds they need. But if businessmen plan too little spending for new plants and equipment, an easing in the cost and availability of money and credit is not likely to lead many of them to change their minds and increase these expenditures. For these reasons, it has been said that monetary policy is like a string: you can hold back with it, but you cannot push with it. The right kind of monetary policy is necessary if we want to stimulate private business spending, but the primary stimulus or drive must come from elsewhere.

A definite upward push can be given to the level of economic activity by the use of another group of tools. These are contained within what is called "fiscal policy," that is, policy dealing with government receipts and expenditures. Fiscal policies have an important bearing upon the total demand for new goods and services. As pointed out earlier, governments are important purchasers of goods and services for public purposes. By changing the level of government spending of this type, the total demand may be increased or decreased directly. But fiscal policy also influences the spending of consumers and businesses. Consumers do their spending and saving out of their incomes after income taxes have been deducted. If income taxes are raised while gross incomes remain unchanged, consumers will have less after-tax income to dispose of as they see fit. When income taxes are cut, this disposable income rises; as a result, consumers may be expected to increase their expenditures for private consumption. Similarly, increases or decreases in corporate profit taxes leave businesses with less or more after-tax earnings which may be used to purchase new plants and equipment. The tax cut of 1964 falls, of course, within the category of fiscal policy.

The taxation side of fiscal policy also has an influence on the growth of productive capacity and thus on the ability of businesses to supply additional output. In deciding whether to build a new plant, it is the profits after taxes which are evaluated to see whether they justify the project. If taxes on corporate profits are reduced, the after-tax earnings of various projects are increased. Some new capacity which did not appear to be worthwhile before the tax cut may now be sufficiently attractive to warrant going ahead with construction. Thus fiscal policy may affect the total supply of goods and services as well as the total demand for them.

The picture of the economic system which we have been developing enables us to put the tax cut in perspective and allows us to understand the results which were expected from it. We should recall that the purpose of the cut was to raise the level of economic activity to the full employment level, which involved increasing the output of new goods and services by some thirty billion dollars. The primary stimulus to accomplish this was contained in the nine billion dollar reduction in income tax payments by individuals, spread over the two-year period. To see the expected results of this action, we must trace several steps.

If income tax payments are reduced by nine billion dollars, the disposable incomes of consumers will be increased by the same amount. In line with their past behavior, consumers may be expected to spend most of this added income for additional goods and services rather than for savings. Thus, in the first step, the tax cut should lead to a rise in consumer demand by something less than nine billion dollars. But the process does not end here. As the total spending for goods and services rises, so does the volume of production and employment. Most of the money received by business from the sale of additional output is paid back to consumers as income in return for the added labor and other resources needed to produce it. This further increase in consumer incomes gives rise to a second step in which the consumers again increase the volume of their spending for goods and services. Although gradually decreasing in size, third, fourth, and fifth steps follow, gradually building up the level of consumer expenditures and productive activity. This process has been called "the multiplier," since the total increase in consumer demand resulting from the tax cut will be some multiple of the initial nine billion dollar increase in disposable incomes.

Just how high this process will carry the level of consumer spending and how long the process will take is uncertain. At each step in the sequence, consumers will save some of their added income rather than spend all of it. As the sales of businesses rise, some of the money will be used to pay higher taxes and for other purposes rather than to be returned to consumers as increased incomes. As consumer incomes are increased, there will again be more income taxes to be paid to the government. These and other factors limit the ultimate rise in consumer demand. In recent testimony before the Joint Economic Committee of the Congress, most witnesses were of the opinion that the multiplier to be applied to the cut in individual income taxes lay between two and two and one-half. From a nine billion reduction in taxes, we could expect that consumer spending would ultimately rise by perhaps eighteen or twenty-two billion dollars. Because of the number of complicating factors which make predicting the future difficult, however, these estimates are not precise.

To some extent, this increase in the level of consumer spending may be expected to induce greater business expenditures for new plants and equipment and additions to inventories. Some companies will run out of idle capacity and will place additional orders for new equipment; others will be encouraged by the higher level of activity to replace old or obsolete equipment with new machines. The cut in corporation taxes, combined with a monetary policy of easy money and credit, should ensure that businesses will be able to finance the added spending. Although some increase in business spending is expected, the amount of the increase cannot be reliably estimated. Once added capacity is built, it is expected to last a long time. In deciding whether it should be built, expectations about the future are often more important than the conditions existing today.

Despite the complexities and uncertainties in the situation, the Council of Economic Advisers to the President made some specific forecasts of the results they expected from the tax cut. In January of 1964 the Council predicted that if the tax reduction program were adopted, the gross national product for the year would rise to 623 billion dollars. As a result of the increase in the level of activity expected, unemployment would fall to about 5% of the labor force. In early 1965, it appeared that these forecasts had been amazingly accurate. The gross national product for 1964 was estimated to be within one billion dollars of the predicted figure. For the month of December, 1964, the reported figure for unemployment was 4.9%. Of course, the accuracy of these forecasts involved a considerable amount of good luck. During the year, there were no major changes in the cold war or other environmental factors to alter the basic situation.

Although as of early 1965 the economy seemed to be expanding according to schedule, we cannot be sure that the tax cuts of 1964 will ultimately accomplish their intended objectives. At the same time that the direct consequences of the tax cut are working themselves out, our economic system and the world of which it is a part will both be changing. New forces and events now completely unforeseen will come into play and raise or lower our level of economic activity. The stimulus to economic activity contained in the tax program may turn out to be greater than necessary or desirable. The total demand for goods and services may rise beyond what we can produce, even with full employment. If this happens, inflationary pressures will exist, and a general rise in prices will be in the offing. It is also possible that this stimulus will be too small to move us to the full employment level of activity. Additional measures may have to be taken to avoid serious unemployment and to enable us to realize our potential. There can be no final solution to the problem of the level of economic activity. As conditions change, further adjustments in the fiscal and monetary policies of the government will be required to keep our economy healthy.

In a relatively free system such as ours, there will always exist sources of potential economic instability. One result of the freedom of choice which our consumers and businesses have—to spend or to save, to invest or not to invest—is that total demand for new goods and services will sometimes be too large and sometimes too small to keep us at full employment. The revolution in economic analysis resulting from the work of Keynes and others has given us knowledge of how to keep the level of economic activity within an acceptable range. Further work by economists in this field will make it possible to refine our policy tools and their usage and to improve the accuracy of economic forecasts. These improvements are some of the results expected from the types of economic research now in progress.

Economic Research and Its Significance

chapter five

Having looked at how economics developed and having surveyed two broad areas of current economics, we now turn to the question of where the field seems to be heading. It is, of course, impossible to foresee future developments either very precisely or very far into the future. At the same time, in a field which is increasingly scientific in method, the next steps depend upon the results of current research. Thus the lines of investigation and the types of research being pursued now are of more than incidental interest.

In economics, as in the other social sciences, there are two basic reasons why research is needed. Our economic system is so complex that a great deal of work needs to be done to improve our understanding of how it functions and what its present capabilities are. In the last two chapters we noted a number of cases in which additional work was needed to help us decide what public policy should be adopted to promote the general welfare. But not all current research is directed toward our immediate public policy problems. In part these efforts have as their aim the improvement of our understanding of economic society generally. Developments in economics itself, together with the advances being made in mathematics, statistics, and other fields of study, are constantly creating new opportunities for the advancement of economic knowledge.

The other major reason for economic research is that the system itself changes. It does not remain static. As economic development occurs, technological advances are made, new forms of business enterprises and improved business methods are introduced, new government programs and agencies are developed, and new possibilities and problems emerge.

At the same time, changes in the political situation of the world impose new requirements on our economy in supporting such activities as defense, foreign aid, and the exploration of space. All of these developments produce, over a period of time, gradual changes in the nature and functioning of our economic system. Much effort is required to keep abreast of these evolutionary changes and to understand their implications.

Since both economics and its subject matter are constantly changing, two separate but related kinds of historical research are necessary. Economic history deals with the evolution of the economic system itself. An understanding of why our present economy is what it is requires that we know the forces and events which molded its development. To the extent that broad trends in the past may be expected to continue in the future, economic history may also give us some notion of the shape of things to come. The history of economic thought, on the other hand, deals with the evolution of economic knowledge and understanding. An improved appreciation of both the strengths and weaknesses of the analytical tools of economics may be gained from studies of how and why these tools developed.

Other types of research deal with the functioning of the economic system as it exists today. Some studies investigate the nature and operation of economic institutions. By the term "institution" we mean, broadly, the cast of actors on the economic stage: consumers, businesses, governments, markets, and other components of the system. Studies of this type may involve the investigation of the kinds of workers who are unemployed, the characteristics of the furniture industry in New England, the organization of the steel workers' union, the types of activities in the federal highway program, changes in international financial markets, or a truly infinite list of other topics.

Another type of study attempts to investigate the current performance of the economic system or of some of its parts. Here the emphasis is on the results obtained, the reasons for them, and their evaluation. What is happening to the level and distribution of consumer incomes, unemployment, the rate of introduction of automated machinery, the amount of technological research in drugs and other chemicals, the number of firms in the automobile industry, the known supplies of petroleum and other fuels, and the international flows of gold and credit? Why are these changes occurring? What do they mean? Is our economic development as rapid as might be expected under present conditions, or are we missing significant opportunities for improvement?

Still another kind of investigation attempts to forecast the future. Forecasting the economic weather is extremely difficult and the accuracy of prediction is not yet very high. However, many public and private decisions made today necessarily involve some prognostication. As pointed out in the last chapter, the tax cut of 1964 was based on the conviction that without it the level of unemployment in the country would be too high. Readings of the future both with and without the tax cut were necessary to decide that this change was desirable. Similarly, each year private industry spends billions of dollars for new buildings and equipment, some of which will last for a long time. On the basis of their predictions, companies are gambling that this new capacity will not become obsolete or useless before their investments have been repaid.

Many studies, including those oriented toward specific public policy problems, combine all of these types of research. To understand a problem, we must know how it developed. The relevant analytical tools and their strengths and weaknesses must be known. The particular characteristics of the economic units involved in the problem must have been established. Both the current performance and our present capabilities in the area are important ingredients in the study of the problem. In evaluating alternative policies, we must have forecasts of the results which will flow from these actions. The efficiency of these studies in providing guides to policy decisions can be no greater than the weakest link of this chain.

The types of research which we have been discussing differ in their purposes. But whether the purpose of the research is to trace some development of the past, to investigate some aspect of the present, or to forecast some part of the future, there are general similarities in the methods used. These common elements reflect the increasingly widespread use of one variety of the scientific method. To be sure, it is generally not possible in economics to make use of the methods of experimental or laboratory sciences. We are not able to remove a family, a business, or a governmental unit from the real world into a laboratory to observe how these would behave under controlled conditions. Yet in a very real sense, the entire economic world is a vast laboratory. All around us economic activity and changes in that activity are taking place. By means of thorough observation and recording of economic events and careful analysis of the information gained, our knowledge of the economic system may be improved. From what has happened, we can gradually establish the characteristics of the economic system and of the forces at work in it.

Thus, economic research involves the analysis of activity which takes place in the constantly changing real world rather than in a laboratory. Yet our economic system is very complex and there are many interrelationships among its parts. As we saw in Chapter Two, the development of a general equilibrium theory emphasized that events in one part of the economy are likely to have both direct and indirect repercussions on many other parts. The fact that we cannot isolate the economic units we are concerned with in a particular project from events occurring in other parts of the economy, makes economic research particularly difficult. Considerable skill and sophistication are required to prevent these extraneous events from obscuring the results for which we are looking.

To handle these intricacies of the economic system adequately, most economic studies must themselves be quite complex. The investigator must obtain information dealing not only with the economic relationship which is the matter of his primary interest, but also on other events and forces likely to bear upon the situation. In deciding what information is relevant, he must draw on our accumulated knowledge of economic institutions and of those general characteristics of economic behavior which we call theory. From this accumulated knowledge and from his own insights, he must suggest hypotheses, or tentative explanations, of the behavior observed. Finally, these hypotheses are tested against the available information and the known characteristics of economic relationships to see whether they can be proved or disproved. In quantitative studies, mathematical and statistical techniques are used in measuring and in isolating the impact of extraneous events as well as in accepting or rejecting the hypotheses. This is the version of the scientific method most useful in economic research.

In the classification of economic research that we have been making up to this point, the stress has been placed on the objective or purpose of the study. There is, however, another subdivision that may be employed in the classification of the kinds of activities in which research economists are engaged. Thus we can distinguish between work in the theoretical and empirical areas. Research in the theoretical area involves the development of new general propositions concerning some aspect of economic behavior and their logical implications. As we have seen in Chapter Two, the work of the classical economists—Smith, Mill, and others—was of a purely theoretical character. The entire picture of the operation of the competitive market economy produced by these economists was deduced from a relatively small set of common sense assumptions. The empirical area of research involves the collection and ordering of economic facts to improve our knowledge of actual economic behavior and to enable the testing of appropriate theoretical hypotheses. As we shall see, this division is not a sharp one and it is one of the important characteristics of contemporary economic thought that efforts are being made to merge more completely the two kinds of research efforts.

As an aid in handling the complex interrelationships involved, many studies make use of what are called "economic models." These models are simplified representations of some aspect or phase of the economic system. With all irrelevant details out of the picture, the models allow us to focus our attention on the most important economic forces and characteristics relevant to our problem.

One kind of model is primarily explanatory or illustrative. Models of this type are used in many fields other than economics. Some of the educational toys which have been developed in recent years fall into this category. A few plastic model cars contain the miniature parts of the power train and show how power is transmitted from the pistons and the drive shaft to turn the rear axles. Models of human anatomy have been developed to illustrate for youngsters the positions of the organs and the relationships of bones and muscles. Some economic models are primarily of this explanatory type. The circular flow diagram in Chapter One is a very simple example.

Other models are more experimental or predictive in character. A common classroom experiment in biological science involves the study of the germination of seeds and the growth of plants. Seeds are planted in different soils, then receive different amounts of water, light, and fertilizers. The speed of germination and the rates of growth of the plants are than related to differences in these factors. The different pots represent a single experimental model into which a variety of conditions have been introduced. The ability of this model to show the impact of the changing conditions introduced into it is what makes this an experimental or predictive model. Similar examples may be found in baking, although these illustrations are not usually thought of as experimental. Doughnut dough containing no leavening agent will produce only hard and inedible rings. By adding yeast to the dough, we obtain bread-like or, as they are usually called, "raised" doughnuts. If instead of yeast we add baking powder, we obtain the common or cake-like doughnut. By studying similar examples, we can draw conclusions about the effects of various leavening agents on doughs.

Models of this experimental or predictive type are widely used in economics. Here, however, most models are made up of a series of mathematical equations. In our biological example, through careful measurement of plant growth under controlled conditions, it is possible to develop an equation which will state how changes in light, moisture, and fertilizer will affect the rate of plant growth. Similarly, many economic relationships may be stated in mathematical terms. If the amount of spending for new goods and services by all consumers in the economy depends upon the current level of consumer incomes, the level of consumer prices, the amount of installment debt which consumers owe, and similar factors, these relationships may be stated in the form of an equation. Each equation in an economic model expresses a set of relationships of this type. Taken altogether, these equations describe the functioning of some part of the economic system.

Although models have been used in economics for a long time, the development of very complex and sophisticated economic models is still in its infancy. This device seems to hold great promise in several areas. In part, the result should be a significant improvement in our forecasts of the economic weather. Forecasting through the use of models has been done for a number of years, but the models used were quite simple. Being simple, they stated the characteristics of the economic system in a rather inadequate fashion. As models are developed which include more precise representations of more of the known characteristics of the economy, the accuracy and reliability of economic forecasts should increase. However, models promise improvements in more than pure forecasting; as more sophisticated models evolve, some use of them as experimental tools is possible. Once a model has been created, by altering one of the conditions within the model or by changing one of the assumptions which reflect the influence of the outside world, we can use the model to answer questions of the speculative type. What if such and so happened? What if this policy were adopted rather than an alternative? Through the use of models, testing techniques analogous to those in the laboratory sciences appear likely to be developed.

As an example of a complex model of the predictive or experimental type, we may consider the report on the inter-industry structure of the U.S. economy, published in 1964 by the Department of Commerce. Pioneered by Professor Wassily Leontief of Harvard University, this type of study attempts to measure the impact of changes in the volume of production in one industry on the level of activity in all other industries. Suppose that consumers increase their purchases of automobiles. Obviously an increase in the production of motor vehicles will require increases in the output of steel, iron ore, coal, tires, copper wire, upholstery fabrics and materials, electricity, and other products. As the industries manufacturing these products expand their outputs, they will require more materials and services from still other parts of the economy. Based on information on the flows of goods and services between industries, models have been developed to measure these inter-industry relationships. During the Korean Conflict a model of this type was used to predict the impact on the economy of the rapid build-up of war material. Potential shortages or bottlenecks could be identified before they occurred. Yet this information is also of value to private companies. In deciding whether or not to build new plants, firms must estimate the future demand for their products. Knowledge of how their products fit into the total picture of production is valuable in making these forecasts.

The Keynesian model of the determinants of the level of income, output, employment, and prices offers an excellent illustration of the ways in which theoretical and empirical research interact. As discussed earlier, Keynes was concerned with the forces which caused variations in the level of activity in the entire economic system. In his work Keynes employed concepts such as total output, total demand, etc. In the early 1930's when he was writing, the available data on these and related matters were quite weak. Thus while Keynes was able to postulate a systematic relationship between the levels of consumer incomes and consumer spending as an important part of his theoretical model, he was not able to measure this relationship with any precision. Yet, in applications of the theory, such as in the prediction of the effects of the tax cut of 1964, an accurate estimate of this relationship is essential. In order to extend, apply, or even challenge the Keynesian framework, a great deal of empirical research was required to provide numerical measures of the quantities involved. Although it had been started by business cycle analysts as early as the 1920's, our present system of National Income and Product Accounts owes much to the stimulus provided by the Keynesian theories. At the same time this expansion in the body of relevant information led to corrections and extensions of the theoretical structure. Our systems for collecting and tabulating data and the theoretical systems associated with them, are constantly in a state of evolution.

Since economic research is so difficult, the efforts of many individuals and of many organizations, both public and private, are necessary to make it possible. Collection and tabulation of economic data are so costly in both time and resources that any great duplication of effort must be avoided. As knowledge about economic institutions and behavior increases, it must be passed on to other workers in the field. When new analytical problems emerge, new tools of mathematical and statistical logic must be made available to handle them. Many diverse and specialized contributions are required for the advancement of economic knowledge.

Although it is unplanned and uncoordinated, a system of economic research has gradually evolved in this country. The system is in some respects rather nebulous, since it is so informal, yet some of its aspects are becoming clear. These involve a kind of division and specialization of labor in the research effort.

During the past thirty years the federal government has increasingly accepted primary responsibility for collecting and publishing economic data. Although the fact is not generally recognized, the collection of economic information has become one of the major functions of many departments of government. Some thirty-eight hundred professional and technical employees and an unknown number of clerical and other workers have a direct part in this information system. Nearly all, if not all, government agencies play some part in the federal statistical program. The Bureau of the Budget contains the central coordinating agency for all of these statistical programs and activities. Nearly all of the figures published are likely to be relevant at some time or other to particular economic studies. Without the information supplied by this elaborate set of programs, economic research would be greatly hampered.

If the federal government has assumed the primary role in the production of economic information, the pioneering work in the development of new types of data and of new systems of measurement has been done largely by private individuals and organizations. Academic economists, both individually and in groups, have generally made the major contributions in this area. The National Bureau of Economic Research, established in 1920 through the cooperative efforts of economists in a number of colleges and universities, is worthy of special mention. This organization led the development of our gross national product figures and participated in the development of other economic measures which have become parts of the federal statistical program. Trade associations (organizations of companies engaged in a particular industry) frequently publish much of the information collected primarily for the benefit of the members of the organization. Since the gathering of information is so expensive that duplication of effort rarely occurs, these various activities, public and private, complement and reinforce each other.

In recent years several kinds of improvements in the data system have been under way. Within the federal government a major effort is being made to weld the statistical programs of the various departments into one system. In the past, each department produced its own figures, with little or no concern for how its information might be combined with that from others. Each agency was likely to have its own concepts, its own definitions, its own system of classifying industries, and its own format for publishing the results. In many cases it was difficult, if not impossible, for researchers to combine in a meaningful way data drawn from different government agencies. Many of these difficulties have been or are being resolved. While improvements in existing programs were in process, new types of data also were being developed. Our economic data have been deficient in the measurement of the national wealth, that inheritance of accumulated capital and other goods from the past which we carry over into the future. The technical problems involved in producing measures of this kind are many and difficult to solve. As a contribution toward solving some of these problems, the National Bureau of Economic Research has recently published a series of studies on the amount of capital accumulated in various parts of the economy and how it is financed. Another area in which our information has been lacking is that of the expectations of consumers and businessmen as to what the future holds for them and what their plans are. As we saw in Chapter Four, these expectations and plans are important in forecasting the future level of activity in the economic system. Considerable effort has been devoted recently to improving our measures of these expectations and in learning how to interpret them.

Although economists have been aware for a long time that improvements in economic data and in analytical methods were highly desirable, many of these developments had to await a technological breakthrough in electronics—the appearance of the large-scale electronic computer. Collecting, tabulating, and analyzing the vast amounts of information necessary simply could not be done otherwise. The mathematical characteristics of complex models can now be systematically explored. Since literally months of work with the best desk calculator available may be compressed into one hour on a computer, many projects which were virtually impossible before are now perfectly feasible. A whole new series of doors to new knowledge are waiting to be opened.

These developments in economics have involved other fields as well. Problems in the economic area have stimulated men in other specialties and the resulting improvements in these related fields have benefited economics. Look at the field of mathematics, for example. Almost a hundred years ago, economists began to use mathematics to state their concepts more clearly and to make their analyses more precise. For the most part, this has involved just the application of existing mathematical tools to economic problems. Starting about two decades ago, it became apparent that these established tools were inadequate in treating some economic problems. New types of mathematical logic would have to be constructed if answers were to be found to some of our economic questions. Largely in response to this need in economics, two new types of tools have already been developed. One of these has been given the rather odd-sounding name of the "theory of games." This type of logic deals with the situation in which two or more individuals or businesses are in competition with each other, yet the number of competitors is small enough so that in deciding what he will do, each participant must take into account the policy or strategy of the others. Based on probability and other forms of complex mathematics, this type of theory can help to decide what to do in given situations. The other type of mathematics which has developed is called "linear programming." For certain types of complex problems which can be represented by linear equations and other expressions, methods based on this logic can help in arriving at the best solutions. Thus, although the use of mathematics in economics is old, the two-way interaction between these fields is quite recent. Future advances in economics will no doubt require other innovations in mathematics and in other fields as well.

As we saw in Chapter Two, the methods used by the classical economists were primarily those of syllogistic logic. From a common sense interpretation of everyday experience, these men drew certain simple assumptions or premises concerning economic behavior and the economic system. Given these assumptions, the results which followed were deducted by pure logic. Under the conditions of the times—the absence of economic data and a general lack of understanding of the scientific method—this was the only feasible approach. Yet the method was a dangerous one: the outcome of the analysis was determined by the assumptions made, and there was no way of testing the validity or applicability of these assumptions. Consequently, classical economics could not be very scientific.

Through the application of refined mathematical and statistical techniques to the increasing amount of information available, a much more scientific approach to economic problems has become possible. The characteristics of the economic system are now being established by the analysis of carefully recorded measures of economic behavior rather than by assumptions. Using the newly developed tools, it is now possible to portray and to study quite complex economic relationships. Laymen may well wonder how rather abstract mechanical models made up of numbers and symbols can do justice to the richness and complexity of human society. Have we lost track of the human element, the importance of the individual? The answer is a loud "No." Paradoxical as it may seem, to promote the welfare of the individuals in our society, the economist is forced by the very complexity of the society to deal in abstractions. In the first chapter we noted that the economic system is itself an abstraction but that it is still very real. If the methods of economics have changed since the time of Adam Smith, the goals or objectives have not. These improvements in methods allow us gradually to reduce the range of the unknown.

Although our understanding is constantly improving, our need for new knowledge will never disappear. As the economy changes and new problems develop, the list of things we need to know grows longer. But if the battle against the unknown may never be wholly won, it is always in danger of being lost. One lesson of history is that failure to solve our economic problems may destroy the fabric of society and the lives of the individuals within it. Unremitting effort is required to gain the knowledge that will enable us to manage adequately the economic aspect of the human situation.

Economic Controversy and Common Concerns

chapter six

> Yet, year in and year out, it is the questions of economics—the manifold issues surrounding collective bargaining, the problems of farm price policy, tariffs, public spending, taxation, and the regulation of business—which provide us with the bread and butter of political controversy. It is these that give us our daily diet of insinuation, indignation, and insult.
>
> JOHN KENNETH GALBRAITH

One could easily add economics to the list of subjects such as sex, religion, and politics that are not supposed to be discussed in polite society. Like these other subjects, economic matters are a persistent source of irritation, uncertainty, and anxiety for most people. Man's economic welfare is a fundamental social objective. Yet questions of what our goals ought to be and how they are best obtained are ones on which differences of opinion and passionate debates can easily occur. Opposing views on the significance of current economic events, the likelihood of future trends, and the desirability of a certain policy are a never ending source of controversy in our public life and social relations. Unfortunately, economic analysis alone cannot, in many instances, provide the "correct" solution to economic problems or eliminate the necessity of making hard choices. It can, however, perform a great service by placing policy questions in proper perspective and focusing attention on essentials so that misdirected controversy is minimized.

In this chapter we shall treat a number of topics that have been a recurrent source of public concern. Our aim is to illustrate how economics and economists enter into the process of resolving disputes over economic issues—not to formulate specific solutions to economic problems. What we are concerned with here is one of the most significant aspects of economics—namely its application in our everyday life.

In a political democracy such as we have in the United States, an individual cannot avoid taking a position on questions of public economic policy. If he does not explicitly take a stand, his silence is taken as implicit approval of what the government does in his name. This places the individual citizen, usually only a passive participant in economic controversy, in something of a dilemma. As a general rule, he does not have the technical knowledge necessary to make his own study of policy questions. On the other hand, he hears statements—by experts, the representatives of various organizations, and politicians—which, although they conflict and lead to different conclusions, seem each to have some merit. How can he decide intelligently? He cannot simply turn the decision over to the expert without surrendering his right to decide for himself what is good and just. But in most instances he cannot do without the services of the expert and some knowledge of economics, because economic problems are difficult and complex affairs. Common sense and personal experience are not an adequate basis for understanding public economic problems. Useless controversy and misdirected economic policy can only be avoided if the citizen is willing to employ economic reasoning when exercising his rights as an individual.

Before proceeding to some of the specific economic issues that are the subject of worry and debate in our society, we should perhaps first consider the various general types of economic controversy that are encountered. This will help us to identify what is basically at stake in the discussion of economic issues. There are three essential elements in all questions of economic policy. First, there must be some view of how our economic system is actually operating and of the results it is producing. Second, there must be some idea of how things ought to be. Finally, there is some proposal as to what, if anything, should be done to make the economy or its results conform to what it ought to be. Controversy may occur over any one or all of these points.

There can be considerable disagreement on questions relating to the current condition and operation of the economy. The questions involved, such as what causes unemployment or whether the economy is realizing its potential rate of growth, are not purely factual. They involve theories of causal relationships and interpretive analysis. It is on these questions that the economists can potentially make their greatest contributions. However, in economics as in other sciences, there is a considerable amount of what might be called technical controversy. This is generated as economists challenge old assumptions and theories with new insights and conceptions derived from the type of research that we reviewed in the last chapter. This technical controversy is often closely related to questions of public policy. Differences in fundamental assumptions about the structure of the economy or the characteristics of economic behavior can be the root of disagreement among economists concerning both the nature of a problem and the alternative ways of resolving it. Fortunately, these technical disputes are scientific and are ultimately settled by greater research efforts on the part of economists. In the short run, however, a lack of adequate data may make it impossible to settle technical disputes conclusively, and economists may remain divided on questions that are crucial to the formulation of public policy. This is not to say that economists always differ; technical disputes at any one time only involve a relatively small number of points in the total body of economics.

George Bernard Shaw was quite unfair when he remarked that even if all the economists in the world were laid end to end, they still would not reach a common conclusion. Laymen are often disturbed by the fact that there always seem to be economists on both sides of a policy dispute. It is difficult to distinguish between the technical controversy associated with the statements made by economists as scientists and the disagreements that arise when economists make statements on public policy as interested individuals. In the latter case the economist is basing his position on his own personal vision of what society can and ought to do. In this regard the economist may serve a useful function as a social architect in making recommendations concerning desirable solutions to economic problems. However, in order to avoid misunderstanding, economists must make clear the personal preconceptions and value judgments that they employ in public debate. When this is done it can easily be seen how economists, who like every one else tend to differ in their individual philosophy and values, can substantially disagree in their recommendations concerning economic policy, even when using the same data and analytic techniques.

A second type of economic controversy involves ideological arguments which are concerned with what *ought* to be. In this case policy issues become the focal point for clashes of doctrinaire positions. An ideology, whether of the capitalist or socialist type, involves preconceived and idealized notions of how things are and how they ought to be. It tends to oversimplify and make all questions strictly one way or the other. Frequently the real economic aspects of public policy issues are forgotten in ideological controversy. For example, the debate on an issue such as government health insurance program for the aged, or even the social security program itself when considered in ideological terms, becomes a question of whether such a program is socialistic or not. A heated trading of slogans or labels does not solve economic problems. At best an ideology may perform a useful function in the discussion of policy programs by providing a simplified and internally consistent view of what is generally desirable in man's economic life. This, however, is only a starting place for the discussion of an economic problem.

A third and final type of economic controversy involves questions of what may be termed political economy. Here the focus is on a particular economic problem and might, for example, involve such questions as whether some of the powers of labor unions should be curbed or whether tariff protection should be granted to an American industry which requests it. The root of the controversy here is the difference in individual or group objectives and interests. In any question of public policy there will be individuals or groups who will be directly benefited and others who will be immediately harmed by the outcome of the issue. The position taken by these people will, as a general rule, be based on their own interests which they will attempt to show are identical with the public interest. Persons not immediately affected by the question will take a position on the basis of what they think is best for society. This judgment may be based on nothing but personal experience, emotion, or prejudice or it may be the result of dispassionate, unbiased analysis of the question from the point of view of the society as a whole.

Frequently the discussion of specific action programs designed to deal with economic problems is complicated by what has been called the "conventional wisdom." This wisdom is composed of the generally accepted ideas and solutions developed in the policy debates of the past. There is a mental inertia on the part of the public which works against any rapid change in accepted ideas. Consequently, there is a strong tendency to apply yesterday's solutions to today's problems. It is the function of the political system of the society to find some compromise of conflicting positions and a workable solution to the economic problem. The persistence of the conventional wisdom greatly complicates this process.

All three forms of controversy are founded on the constant changes that are occurring in human behavior. As man's control of his life and environment continues to expand and improve, there are changes in our understanding of economic behavior, our goals and ideals, and the possibility of consciously influencing economic events. In order to realize the potential that these changes create, there must be an adjustment in the social arrangements by which men live. In the economic sphere, where the change has been especially rapid, there is a strong tendency for the world to move on and the process of social adjustment to lag behind. It is this tendency to lag that is the source of much of the tension that we observe in our political economic life and which from time to time finds its expression in revolutionary changes.

The three types of economic controversy—technical, ideological, and political—are not, of course, mutually exclusive. Elements of all three are usually found in the discussion of any national economic problem. In order to be able to deal intelligently with the problem of policy making and avoid useless controversy, one must be able to recognize the various elements encountered. This is not always easy to do and for the non-economist it is frequently the most difficult part of his participation in economic debate. Therefore, we shall examine some of the economic problems that seem especially to worry people and separate the various strands of argument in order to indicate the manner in which economic understanding can be helpful in thinking about these problems.

For almost a century the tariff has been a subject which has periodically troubled people. The question of a tariff generally arises and is hotly debated when certain industries or groups of workers are subject to severe foreign competition. Pressure is then put on the government to protect the domestic industry by placing a tax on the foreign goods that would price them out of our market. Claims that foreigners are taking American jobs or that cheap foreign labor is unfair competition for American industry are frequently heard in the tariff debate. The arguments for the tariff are generally arguments of interest. But whose interest? An economist, in approaching the question of a tariff, is concerned with the interest or welfare of the society as a whole. When viewed in this way, the tariff issue appears much different than it does to the worker or industry suffering from foreign competition.

From an economic point of view the tariff question leads directly to the broader issue of the very existence of foreign trade. If one industry is to be protected, why not protect them all? The guiding principle in foreign trade, as in purely domestic trade, is that we seek the greatest return for the smallest outlay, i.e., we attempt to economize on the use of our resources. No one would seriously debate the advisability of importing those goods that we cannot produce ourselves or whose production would have an absolutely prohibitive cost: growing bananas in New England greenhouses rather than importing them from South America, for example. A difficulty arises, however, when we recognize that many of the goods that are imported could easily be produced domestically. The situation is analogous to that of a nimble-fingered surgeon who is also a world champion typist but decides to hire a secretary. The surgeon's reasoning in hiring someone less skilled to do his typing is that this frees him to devote all his energy to his surgical practice. There his earning power is so great that he can make sufficient extra income to pay the secretary and still have more left for himself. Applying this same principle, which economists have termed comparative advantage, to the trade of nations, it pays the United States, even if we are generally more efficient than other nations, to specialize in the production of those goods in which we are relatively more efficient and trade them to foreigners for the goods that we are relatively less efficient in producing. As in the case of the surgeon, this will make our total income greater. As a result of this reasoning economists have generally opposed tariffs on the grounds that they tend to reduce the society's total income. For example, when the Congress passed the Hawley-Smoot tariff bill in 1930, 1,028 economists signed petitions protesting the action.

There is another aspect of the nation's international economic relations that in recent times has been and for a considerable time in the future probably will be a topic of much concern in the United States. The fact that since the mid-1950's the nation has been incurring substantial annual deficits on its balance of payments with foreign nations, which reduced our holdings of gold by nine billion dollars, has caused a considerable shock to many Americans. Although many are not sure what this means, it certainly sounds bad. The words deficit and debt have strong ethical and emotional connotations. The immediate impression created by the term deficit in the international balance of payments is that the United States has been importing too many goods from foreign countries. This false impression, and much of the difficulty and confusion encountered in the attempt to formulate an international economic policy designed to cope with the balance-of-payments problem, is the result of unfamiliarity with the tools of economic analysis which are used in stating and thinking about the problem.

The balance of payments is an accounting statement used to sum up the payments and claims to payment that result from a nation's international economic transactions. These transactions are divided into three main categories or classes of accounts. First, there is the current account in which are recorded the payments and claims that result from the export and import of goods and services, private gifts, and government grants. Next, there is the capital account which records the international purchase and sale of real and financial assets and the borrowing and lending transactions between the United States and all other nations. Finally, there is the gold account that records the import and export of gold. It is the gold account that is the nucleus of the balance-of-payments problem. Whenever the current and capital accounts together as a total do not balance, the difference shows up in the gold account. A deficit on the balance of payments exists when gold flows out of the country to compensate for an imbalance in the other payments. Because of the limited supply of gold, sooner or later the imbalance must be corrected. The seriousness of the balance-of-payments problem arises from the fact that the means by which this adjustment is accomplished could have very serious consequences for the level of income and employment in the United States and the rest of the world.

When the United States' balance of payments is examined in detail, it becomes apparent that contrary to what might be expected, the United States' exports of goods and services are much greater than imports. On the other hand, the result of government expenditures for military and foreign aid purposes along with the net balance of private lending and investment overseas exceeds the surplus of our exports over imports of goods and services. Now, what is the cause of the balance-of-payments deficit? To select any one of the elements in the balance of payments as the cause is extremely difficult and there has been considerable disagreement on this point. Even without an exact answer as to which is the cause, a knowledge of the balance of payments does suggest a number of possible alternative solutions to the problem; either increase the export surplus or decrease private lending and/or the government's foreign spending. A variety of specific means are available to accomplish each of these major kinds of readjustment. The best solution depends on a host of factors other than the purely economic ones.

The balance-of-payments problem illustrates a situation that is frequently encountered when dealing with economic problems. A knowledge of economics allows us to make a more detailed statement of the problem, but it does not give us a simple clear-cut answer as to what should be done to solve the problem. The value of the economic analysis in such a case is that it expands the possible choices open to us, even if it does not make the selection of one any easier.

We shall turn now to a purely domestic problem. If one were to judge from the amount of space devoted to it in newspapers and popular magazines, the process of automation troubles people very much. The problem stems from relatively recent technological developments that have made it possible to use automatic control devices, such as computers, to link together the various stages of production into one continuous operation. In an automated process machines operate without constant human supervision. What many find alarming about automation is that machines are replacing men on a large scale. This raises the specter of technological unemployment. For the worker who is displaced and for his union, automation is bad because it has eliminated a job. If the rate at which automated processes are being adopted were to accelerate rapidly this might pose a serious threat of widespread unemployment and possibly even depression. Should the process be stopped before there is a disaster?

Economists are far less alarmed about automation. First viewed from the perspective of economic history, the labor-saving aspect of automation can hardly be considered a new development. The introduction of production line methods involved a similar type of change. Automation is simply the latest form of the kind of technological change which underlies the steady rise in our level of living. To consume more per person we must produce more per person. Labor-saving devices are one important means of doing this. Thus, when one considers its ultimate rather than immediate effect, automation holds a promise of great increase in our national income. According to an idealized view of the operation of the market economy, the price system should operate in such a way that in the long run displaced workers are automatically absorbed in other parts of the economy. In reality, however, the market mechanism does not always work rapidly and efficiently in this regard. In addition, we are less tolerant of inflicting severe social and economic hardship on a particular group in order to benefit society. Economic reasoning would seem to indicate that, if we are determined to prevent undue hardship to workers as a result of automation, the government should intervene and assist in finding new jobs for displaced workers, but should not attempt to prevent automation. Whether this might actually be done depends on the nation's ideological position and a value judgment reflecting whether it is believed that government inter-vention in the operation of the market economy is less undesirable than the hardship for workers caused by the process of automation. There is, of course, no scientific way of weighing these two alternative positions. Economics can only point out that one can only be had at the cost of the other.

One of the difficulties with economic problems is their complexity. The problem of automation, for example, is knotty enough in itself, but unfortunately it has further ramifications of the utmost importance. Technological change, of which automation is a particular example, is a vital ingredient in the process of economic growth. A high level of technological unemployment would, however, tend to slow the rate of growth of output. Now to complete the circle, the problem of tech-nological unemployment is much less severe in a rapidly growing econ-omy where there is a strong demand for labor. As was pointed out in Chapter Four, there has been a tendency in recent years for the rate of economic growth in the United States to slow down and for the average level of unemployment to be relatively high. This situation has stimu-lated concern and discussion of the need and desirability for a more rapid rate of economic growth and the ways in which it might be obtained. This, it will be remembered, was the issue at the heart of the discussion of the tax cut of 1964.

Two opposing positions have appeared in the discussion of the problem of economic growth in the United States. On the one hand, there is a group who may be labeled the stagnationists. Their position is that the slowing of the rate of growth in the United States and the rise in the level of unemployment are the result of insufficient demand for output. This group advocated the tax cut as a means of stimulating the economy. On the other hand, there is a group that can be labeled the structuralists because of the emphasis they place on the inability of the economy to adjust to the technological and other qualitative changes that are part of the growth process. This group did not deny that the tax cut would stimulate spending by the public, but they did question whether this would accelerate the growth process. According to the structuralist view, the root of the problem is the pockets of unemploy-ment and depressed areas that result from the inability of the economy to adjust rapidly as new industries develop and replace old ones and automation displaces workers. This is an example of what we have termed technical controversy. In order to settle the debate between the two schools of thought, it would be necessary to measure accurately the relative importance of these two causes of unemployment. Since at the moment this cannot be done and growth is a politically live issue, the government has attempted to protect itself by taking actions consistent with both positions. In addition to the tax cut there was a so-called area redevelopment act that aimed at retraining and re-employing workers affected by automation and declining industries. In this case, although economic reasoning could not give a single unequivocal answer, policy action did not have to wait upon settling the technical controversy.

There is another issue closely related to the tax cut of 1964 that is a good example of the conventional wisdom. The discussion of government finance invariably involves the question of the government's budget deficit and the national debt. The size of the debt is often a subject of very heated debate. Much of the emotion and concern is the result of the uncritical extension of the tried and proved rules of household finance to the accounts of the government. Steadily rising debt is generally thought to be a sign of mismanagement and impending disaster to a householder. Judging from private practice, the ideal rule for government finance would be a balanced budget.

This view, however, fails to recognize that the national debt is fundamentally different from personal debt in both nature and function. One basic difference is that a government has the power to create both money and income with which to repay its debt. Taxes could be raised to a point where over the next decade or so the debt could be greatly reduced if government expenditures were held constant. Why is this not done? As we saw in Chapter Four, the difference between government receipts and income is a net addition or subtraction from the total demand for goods. An attempt to drive down the level of the debt would have a strong tendency to reduce the level of spending in the economy. This would be fine in a period of excess demand and inflation, but in other circumstances it could cause or certainly aggravate a depression.

The demand for the government to balance its budget at all times and avoid going into debt is founded ultimately on the theory that the economic system is self-adjusting and that government intervention in order to maintain income and employment is unnecessary. Yet, according to the economic reasoning that is currently accepted by the majority of economists, there is no reason why demand will be maintained at just the level required for full employment of our resources. Taken from this point of view the government's deficit and debt are the cost of maintaining full employment. Debt is not the equivalent of red ink marking a loss if it results in the production of goods and the employment of labor that would otherwise not have occurred. In deciding on the advisability of a government deficit one must consider its ultimate purpose and probable effect if it is to be judged on economic grounds. Conventional wisdom, which is based on personal experience and immediate effects, does not do this.

The bulk of the existing public debt in the United States was incurred during periods of depression and war when government deficits in these extreme circumstances were unavoidable and economically justifiable. However, even in more normal times government debt may be justified. Government borrowing, like private business debt, can be incurred for the purpose of purchasing a capital asset. When the proceeds of a government bond issue are used for purposes such as the construction of roads and schools, there is an addition to the nation's wealth and a stream of future services is generated. Just as it may be the most intelligent and sound choice for a business to finance a new plant by borrowing rather than limiting its investment in any one year to the amount that can be financed out of current profits, it is economically feasible for the government to borrow to create new social capital. Thus, contrary to the conventional wisdom, a deficit on the government's budget need not mean that we are living beyond our social means.

Our brief review of some of the economic problems currently troubling Americans and the types of controversy associated with the attempt to formulate public policy to deal with these problems, suggests certain general conclusions concerning the role of economic understanding in the everyday life of our society. The basic economic problem of scarcity can never be solved once and for all. In our dynamic world we are constantly being confronted with new situations, new problems, new knowledge, new potentials, and new aspirations which require continuous adjustment and readjustment in economic matters. Economic understanding is necessary if we are to deal intelligently with these changes.

In order for men to live harmoniously in society, an individual should have both a reasonable knowledge of the operations of the economic system, a clear recognition of the goals he wants to achieve, and make a reasoned choice of the line of action which will best achieve individual and social goals. A knowledge of economics permits the individual citizen to recognize those parts of economic questions for which a "scientific" answer is possible, those for which such answers are impossible because the necessary information or data are unavailable, and those where value judgments are unavoidable. The function of the economist is not to provide answers to ethical or value questions, but only to identify such problems and place them in sharp focus so that intelligent choices can be made. Economics is an important and necessary tool in man's attempt to improve the quality of his life and a knowledge of its contents should be part of the basic education of every citizen.

Suggested Readings and Classroom Materials

TEXTS

Bach, George Leland. *Economics. An Introduction to Analysis and Policy.* Fourth edition. Englewood Cliffs, New Jersey: Prentice-Hall, Inc., 1963.

McConnell, Campbell R. *Economics: Principles, Problems, and Policies.* Second edition. New York: McGraw-Hill Book Company, Inc., 1963.

Samuelson, Paul A. *Economics. An Introductory Analysis.* Sixth edition. New York: McGraw-Hill Book Company, Inc., 1964.

ADDITIONAL READINGS

Balassa, Bela (ed.). *Changing Patterns in Foreign Trade and Payments.* In Norton Series *Problems of the Modern Economy.* New York: W. W. Norton & Company, Inc., 1964.

Bernstein, Peter L. *A Primer on Money, Banking, and Gold.* New York: Vintage Books, 1965.

Boulding, Kenneth. *Principles of Economic Policy.* Englewood Cliffs, New Jersey: Prentice-Hall, Inc., 1958.

Bowen, William G. (ed.). *Labor and the National Economy.* In Norton Series *Problems of the Modern Economy.* New York: W. W. Norton & Company, Inc., 1965.

Campbell, Robert W. *Soviet Economic Power. Its Organization, Growth, and Challenge.* Boston: Houghton Mifflin Company, 1960.

Committee for Economic Development. *Economics Education in the Schools.* A Report of the National Task Force on Economic Education, September, 1961. New York: Committee for Economic Development, 1961.

————. *Economic Literacy for Americans.* New York: Committee for Economic Development, 1962.

Duesenberry, James S. *Money and Credit: Impact and Control.* In *Foundations of Modern Economics Series.* Englewood Cliffs, New Jersey: Prentice-Hall, Inc., 1964.

Ebenstein, William. *Today's Isms. Communism, Fascism, Capitalism, Socialism.* Fourth edition. Englewood Cliffs, New Jersey: Prentice-Hall, Inc., 1964.

Galbraith, John Kenneth. *Economics and the Art of Controversy.* New York: Vintage Books, 1959.

Gutman, Peter M. (ed.). *Economic Growth. An American Problem.* Englewood Cliffs, New Jersey: Prentice-Hall, Inc., 1964.

Hansen, Alvin H. *Economic Issues of the 1960's.* In *Economics Handbook Series.* New York: McGraw-Hill Book Company, Inc., 1960.

————. *The Postwar American Economy. Performance and Problems.* New York: W. W. Norton & Company, Inc., 1964.

Hathaway, Dale E. *Problems of Progress in the Agricultural Economy.* Scott, Foresman & Company, 1964.

Hamovitch, William (ed.). *The Federal Deficit. Fiscal Imprudence or Policy Weapon?* In *Studies in Economics Series.* Boston: D. C. Heath and Company, 1965.

Heilbroner, Robert L. *The Making of Economic Society.* Englewood Cilffs, New Jersey: Prentice-Hall, Inc., 1962.

————. *The Worldly Philosophers.* Revised edition. New York: Simon and Schuster, Inc., 1961.

Heilbroner, Robert L. and Peter L. Bernstein. *A Primer on Government Spending.* New York: Vintage Books, 1963.

Mansfield, Edwin (ed.). *Monopoly Power and Economic Performance.* In Norton Series *Problems of the Modern Economy.* New York: W. W. Norton & Company, Inc., 1964.

Mark, Shelley M. and Daniel M. Slate (eds.). *Economics in Action. Readings in Current Economic Issues.* Second edition. Belmont, California: Wadsworth Publishing Company, Inc., 1962.

Okun, Arthur M. (ed.). *The Battle Against Unemployment.* In Norton Series *Problems of the Modern Economy.* New York: W. W. Norton & Company, Inc., 1965.

Phelps, Edmund S. (ed.). *Private Wants and Public Needs.* Revised edition. In Norton Series *Problems of the Modern Economy.* New York: W. W. Norton & Company, Inc., 1962.

Slesinger, Reuben E. and Asher Isaacs (eds.). *Contemporary Economics. Selected Readings.* Boston: Allyn and Bacon, Inc., 1963.

Vatter, Harold G. *The U.S. Economy in the 1950's. An Economic History.* New York: W. W. Norton & Company, Inc., 1963.
Wilcox, Clark, Willis D. Weatherford, Jr., and Holland Hunter. *Economies of the World Today: Their Organization, Development, and Performance.* New York: Harcourt, Brace & World, Inc., 1962.

CLASSROOM MATERIAL

Reading list from CED. *Economic Literacy for Americans.* New York: Committee for Economic Development, 1962, pp. 40–50. By permission of the Committee.

PART ONE

Production and Its Control Through Markets

A. Approach to Economic Problems

1. WHAT ARE ECONOMIC PROBLEMS? *A Primer of Economics No. 1, by Lewis E. Wagner, Bureau of Business and Economic Research, State University of Iowa, Iowa City, Iowa, 1958 . . . 19pp. . . . 50¢*

2. THE GOALS OF ECONOMIC POLICY. *Report of the Committee on Economic Policy, Economic Research Department, Chamber of Commerce of the United States, 1615 H Street, N.W., Washington 6, D.C., 1961 . . . 35pp. . . . 50¢ (pp. 1–17 only)*

B. Economic Resources (Natural, Human and Capital)

3. NATURAL RESOURCE USE IN OUR ECONOMY *by William H. Stead, Joint Council on Economic Education, 2 West 46th Street, New York 36, N. Y., Revised edition 1960 . . . 36pp. (student edition) . . . 50¢*

4. THE SUPPLY OF RAW MATERIALS. *Chapter 3 (pp. 39–58), Problems of American Economic Growth, by Bruce R. Morris, Oxford University Press, 417 Fifth Avenue, New York, N. Y., 1961 . . . 279pp. . . . $2.50 (Excerpt in preparation.)*

5. THE ADEQUACY OF RESOURCES FOR ECONOMIC GROWTH IN THE UNITED STATES. *Study Paper No. 13, by Joseph L. Fisher and Edward Boorstein, Joint Economic Committee (Study of Employment Growth and Price Levels). U. S. Government Printing Office, Washington, D. C., December 16, 1959 . . . 35pp. . . . 25¢*

6. THE ROLE OF POPULATION, *Chapter 14, and* POPULATION AND LIVING LEVELS, *Chapter 15, Economic Development, by Henry H. Villard. Holt, Rinehart and Winston, Inc., 383 Madison Avenue, New York 17, N. Y., 1959 . . . Complete book . . . $2.50, Chapters above . . . 50¢*

7. BUSINESS IMPLICATIONS OF POPULATION GROWTH *by Philip M. Hauser. Reprint, Business Horizons, Vol. III, No. 2, Summer, 1960, Indiana University, Bloomington, Ind., $1.00*

8. CAPITAL: KEY TO PROGRESS. *Basic Economics, The Industrial Relations Center, The University of Chicago, Chicago 37, Illinois, 1952 . . . 34pp. . . . 50¢*

C. Organization of Business Firms

9. BUSINESS AND THE AMERICAN WAY *by Edward L. Korey. Oxford Social Studies Pamphlets, Oxford Book Company, Inc., 71 Fifth Avenue, New York, N. Y., 1955 . . . revised 1961 . . . 76pp. . . . 65¢ (pp. 1–33)*

10. HOW A CORPORATION WORKS. *Good Reading Rack Service Division, Koster-Dana Corp., 76 Ninth Avenue, New York 11, N. Y., 1960 . . . 15pp. . . . 25¢*

D. Productivity and Technological Change

11. HOW TO RAISE REAL WAGES. *A Statement on National Policy by the Research and Policy Committee of the Committee for Economic Development, 711 Fifth Avenue, New York 22, N. Y., Reprint 1961 . . . 38pp. . . . 50¢*

12. WHAT PRODUCTIVITY MEANS TO EACH OF US *by Jules Backman, The Pure Oil News, Vol. 42, No. 8, January, 1960. Birk & Co., Inc., 3 West 57th Street, New York 19, N. Y. . . . 25¢*

13. PRODUCTIVITY *by Peter O. Steiner and William Goldner, Institute of Industrial Relations, University of California, Berkeley, California, 1952 . . . 60pp. . . . 50¢*

14. AUTOMATION: ITS IMPACT ON ECONOMIC GROWTH AND STABILITY *by Almarin Phillips, American Enterprise Association, Inc., 1012 Fourteenth Street, N.W., Washington 5, D. C., January, 1957 . . . 36pp. . . . (Price on request.)*

15. AUTOMATION: TECHNOLOGY'S NEW FACE *by Jack Rogers, Institute of Industrial Relations, University of California, Berkeley, California, 1958 . . . 94pp. . . . 50¢*

16. AUTOMATION AND TECHNOLOGICAL CHANGE. *Report of the Subcommittee on Economic Stabilization to the Joint Committee on the Economic Report, U. S. Government Printing Office, Washington, D. C., 1955 . . . 13pp. . . . (Price on request.)*

E. Consumer Demand

17. THE CONSUMER'S DOLLAR *by Thomas E. Mullaney. A Current Affairs Publication of The New York Times Office of Educational Activities, 229 West 43rd Street, New York 36, N. Y., January, 1960 . . . 15pp. . . . Free*

18. HOW AMERICAN BUYING HABITS CHANGE. *U. S. Department of Labor, U. S. Government Printing Office, Washington 25, D. C., 1959 . . . 235pp. . . . $1.00*

19. THE ECONOMIC ASPECTS OF ADVERTISING *by Nicholas Kaldor, Chapter 34, Readings in Current Economics, edited by Morton C. Grossman, Reed R. Hansen, et al. Richard D. Irwin, Inc., Homewood, Illinois, 1961 . . . 486pp. . . . $4.50*

F. Operation of a Market System

20. COMPETITIVE PRICES IN ACTION. *Basic Economics, The Industrial Relations Center, The University of Chicago, Chicago 37, Illinois, 1958 . . . 30pp. . . . 50¢*

21. HOW THE AMERICAN ECONOMY IS ORGANIZED. *A Primer of Economics, No. 2, by Clark C. Bloom, Bureau of Business and Economic Research, State University of Iowa, Iowa City, Iowa . . . 34pp. . . . $1.00*

22. A PRISONER OF WAR CAMP *by R. A. Radford, General Economics: A Book of Readings, edited by Thomas J. Anderson, Jr., Abraham L. Gitlow and Daniel E. Diamond. Richard D. Irwin, Inc., Homewood, Illinois, 1959 . . . 487pp. . . . $3.95*

G. Monopoly and Public Policies

23. BUSINESS AND THE AMERICAN WAY *by Edward L. Korey. Oxford Social Studies Pamphlets, Oxford Book Company, Inc., 71 Fifth Avenue, New York, N. Y., 1955 . . . revised, 1961 . . . 76pp. . . . 65¢ (pp. 33–76)*

24. THE CONSUMER AND ANTITRUST *by Jules Joskow and Irwin M. Stelzer, Consumer Problem Series No. 4, Council on Consumer Information, Colorado State College, Greeley, Colorado, 1957 . . . 31pp. . . . 50¢*

Distribution of Income

A. Patterns of Income Distribution

25. PERSONAL DISTRIBUTION *by E. T. Weiler, excerpt from General Economics, A Book of Readings, edited by Thomas J. Anderson, Jr., Abraham L. Gitlow and Daniel E. Diamond. Richard D. Irwin, Inc., Homewood, Illinois, 1959 . . . 487pp. . . . $3.95 . . . Excerpt price 52¢*

26. AMERICA'S HAVES AND HAVE NOTS. *Labor's Economic Review, Vol. 5, No. 8, August, 1960, AFL-CIO Department of Research, AFL-CIO Building, 815 Sixteenth St., N.W., Washington 6, D. C. . . . 25¢*

B. Profits, Wages, and Unions

27. PRICES, PROFITS AND WAGES, A STUDY IN ECONOMIC PRINCIPLES AND HUMAN WELL-BEING. *The American Competitive Enterprise Economy, Pamphlet No. VIII, Chamber of Commerce of the United States, 1615 H Street, N.W., Washington 6, D. C., 1953 . . . 33pp. . . . 50¢*

28. WAGE POLICY FOR AN EXPANDING ECONOMY. *Labor's Economic Review, Vol. 5, No. 11, November, 1960, AFL-CIO Dept. of Research, AFL-CIO Building, 815 Sixteenth Street, N.W., Washington 6, D. C. . . . 25¢*

29. PROFITS AT WORK. *Everyday Economics No. 6, Industrial Relations Center, The University of Chicago, Chicago 37, Ill., 1954 . . . 26pp. . . . 50¢*

30. OUR LABOR FORCE. *Economic Series 53, by Lawrence Senesh and Barbara Warne Newell. Curriculum Resources, Inc., 1515 W. Lake Street, Minneapolis 8, Minn., 1961 . . . 84pp. . . . $1.00*

31. MINIMUM WAGE LAWS. *Bulletin 43, by Donald E. Cullen; New York State School of Industrial and Labor Relations, Cornell University, Ithaca, N. Y., February, 1961 . . . 58pp. . . . 50¢*

Inflation, Recession, and Stabilization Policies

A. Measuring Economic Performance

32. HOW EVERYBODY MAKES A LIVING. *Good Reading Rack Service, Koster-Dana Corp., 76 Ninth Avenue, New York 11, N. Y., 1959 . . . 16pp. . . . 25¢*

33. THE NATIONAL INCOME AND ITS DISTRIBUTION. *A Study in Economic Principles and Human Well-Being, The American Competitive Enterprise Economy, No. IV, Chamber of Commerce of the United States, 1615 H Street, N.W., Washington 6, D. C., 1959 . . . 27pp. . . . 50¢*

34. MEASURING THE PERFORMANCE OF THE ECONOMY. *A Primer of Economics No. 3, by Lewis E. Wagner, Bureau of Business and Economic Research, State University of Iowa, Iowa City, Iowa, July, 1956 . . . 39pp. . . . $1.00*

B. Spending Behavior and Causes of Instability

35. PROSPERITY AND DEPRESSION. *Chapter 6 (pp. 165–183), from Economic Reasoning, by Marshall A. Robinson, Herbert C. Morton, and James D. Calderwood. The Brookings Institution, 1775 Massachusetts Avenue, N.W., Washington 6, D. C., 1959 . . . 335pp. . . . $3.00 . . . Excerpt price . . . 25¢*

36. INCOME, EMPLOYMENT AND PRICES. *A Primer of Economics No. 4,* by Lewis E. Wagner, *Bureau of Business and Economic Research, State University of Iowa, Iowa City, Iowa, September, 1960 . . . 43pp. . . . $1.00*

37. INFLATION: ITS CAUSES AND EFFECTS by Carroll E. Daugherty, *Bell Telephone Magazine, Vol. XXXVII, No. 4, Winter 1958–59, Public Relations Dept., American Telephone & Telegraph Co., 195 Broadway, New York 7, N. Y. . . . Free*

38. UNEMPLOYMENT: IS PERMANENT PREVENTION POSSIBLE? *Vital Issues, Vol. VIII, No. 10, Center for Information on America, Washington, Conn., June, 1959 . . . 35¢*

39. PRICING IN AN ADMINISTERED ECONOMY by A. E. Kahn, *Georgia Business, Vol. 19, No. 5, November, 1959, College of Business Administration, The University of Georgia, Athens, Georgia. (Price on request.)*

40. ECONOMIC REPORT OF THE PRESIDENT. *January, 1961, U. S. Government Printing Office, Washington, D. C. . . . 214pp. . . . $1.00*

41. THE CONSUMER PRICE INDEX, A SHORT DESCRIPTION. *January, 1959, U. S. Department of Labor, Bureau of Labor Statistics, Washington 25, D. C. . . . 11pp. . . . (Price on request.)*

C. Money, Banking and Monetary Policies

42. MONEY AND BANKING IN THE AMERICAN ECONOMY by Weldon Welfling, *CASE Economic Literacy Series No. 3, Council for the Advancement of Secondary Education, 1201 Sixteenth St., N.W., Washington 6, D. C., 1960 . . . 104pp. . . . $1.00*

43. MONEY: MASTER OR SERVANT? by Thomas O. Waage, *Federal Reserve Bank of New York, 33 Liberty Street, New York 45, N. Y., May, 1955 . . . Free*

44. UNDERSTANDING MONEY AND BANKING. *Basic Economics, The Industrial Relations Center, The University of Chicago, Chicago 37, Illinois, 1953 . . . 31pp. . . . 50¢*

45. MODERN MONEY MECHANICS. *A Workbook on Deposits, Currency and Bank Reserves, Federal Reserve Bank of Chicago, Chicago 90, Illinois, May, 1961 . . . 31pp. . . . Free*

46. THE FEDERAL RESERVE AT WORK. *Annual Report 1960, Federal Reserve Bank of Richmond, Richmond 13, Virginia . . . 32pp. . . . (1–14 and 22–25 only) . . . Free*

47. THE FEDERAL RESERVE SYSTEM: PURPOSES AND FUNCTIONS. *Board of Governors of the Federal Reserve System, Washington 25, D. C., 1961 . . . 238pp. . . . Free*

D. Fiscal Policies
48. THE STABILIZING BUDGET POLICY: WHAT IT IS AND HOW IT WORKS. *Committee for Economic Development, 711 Fifth Avenue, New York 22, N. Y., July, 1950 . . . 24pp. . . . 30¢*
E. Role of Debt
49. DEBT: PUBLIC AND PRIVATE. *Report of the Committee on Economic Policy, Chamber of Commerce of the United States, 1615 H Street, N.W., Washington 6, D. C., 1961 . . . 47pp. . . . $1.00*
50. THE NATIONAL DEBT AS A "BURDEN" *by Wallace E. Ogg. Farm Policy Forum, Vol. 6, No. 4, April, 1953, The Iowa State College Press, Ames, Iowa . . . (Price on request.)*
51. THE ROLE OF THE DEBT IN OUR ECONOMY *by Robert H. Johnson. Farm Policy Forum, Vol. 6, No. 4, April, 1953, The Iowa State College Press, Ames, Iowa . . . (Price on request.)*

PART TWO—The material listed here is presented as broad, major areas of study which cut across the analytical classifications of Part One. These areas of study provide numerous opportunities to use concepts and principles developed in the materials above.

Special Areas of Study

A. Agriculture
52. THE FARM PROBLEM IDENTIFIED *by Wallace Barr, The Farm Problem—What Are The Choices? No. 1, National Committee on Agricultural Policy, The Ohio State University, Columbus, Ohio . . . 6pp. . . . (Price on request.)*
53. NATURE OF THE FARM PROBLEM *by Earl O. Heady, Adjustments in Agriculture—A National Basebook, Iowa State University Press, Ames, Iowa, 1961 . . . 376pp. . . . $3.95*
54. FARM POLICY FOR THE SIXTIES *by Lauren K. Soth, Chapter 9, Goals for Americans. The Report of the President's Commission on National Goals, Prentice-Hall, Inc., Englewood Cliffs, N. J., 1960 . . . 372pp. . . . $1.00*
55. WHAT MAKES FARMER'S PRICES *by Wayne Dexter, Agriculture Bulletin 204, U. S. Dept. of Agriculture. U. S. Government Printing Office, Washington 25, D. C., April, 1959 . . . 22pp. . . . 20¢*
56. THE FARM PROBLEM—WHAT ARE THE CHOICES? *A series of leaflets prepared by the National Committee on Agricultural Policy, The Ohio State University, Columbus, Ohio . . . (Price on request.)*

57. ADJUSTMENTS IN AGRICULTURE—A NATIONAL BASEBOOK. *Mervin G. Smith and Carlton F. Christian (eds.), Iowa State University Press, Ames, Iowa, 1961 . . . 376pp. . . . $3.95*

B. Public Finance

58. FEDERAL TAXES—STATE AND LOCAL TAXES. *A handbook on problems and solutions, AFL-CIO Publication Nos. 80 and 108 combined, AFL-CIO Building, 815 Sixteenth Street, N.W., Washington 6, D. C. . . . 22pp. . . . 50¢*

59. THE TAXES WE PAY *by Maxwell S. Stewart, Public Affairs Pamphlet No. 289, Public Affairs Committee, Inc., 22 East 38th Street, New York 16, N. Y., October, 1959 . . . 27pp. . . . 25¢*

60. THE ROLE OF THE DEBT IN OUR ECONOMY *by Robert H. Johnson, Farm Policy Forum, Vol. 6, No. 4, April, 1953, The Iowa State College Press, Ames, Iowa . . . (Price on request.)*

61. THE NATIONAL DEBT AS A "BURDEN" *by Wallace E. Ogg, Farm Policy Forum, Vol. 6, No. 4, April, 1953, The Iowa State College Press, Ames, Iowa . . . (Price on request.)*

62. DEBT: PUBLIC AND PRIVATE. *Economics Research Department, Chamber of Commerce of the United States, 1615 H Street, N.W., Washington 6, D. C., 1961 . . . 47pp. . . . $1.00*

63. THE STABILIZING BUDGET POLICY: WHAT IT IS AND HOW IT WORKS. *Committee for Economic Development, 711 Fifth Avenue, New York 22, N. Y., July, 1950 . . . 24pp. . . . 30¢*

64. THE FEDERAL BUDGET IN BRIEF, 1962. *Bureau of the Budget, Executive Office of the President, U. S. Government Printing Office, Washington 25, D. C., January, 1961 . . . 62pp. . . . 25¢*

C. Economic Security and Welfare Programs

65. ECONOMIC SECURITY FOR AMERICANS, AN ANALYSIS. *Joint Council on Economic Education, 2 West 46th Street, New York 36, N. Y., 1955 . . . 52pp. . . . 65¢*

66. SOME ECONOMIC IMPLICATIONS OF WELFARE PROGRAMS *by Robert H. Johnson, Iowa Business Digest, Vol. 25, No. 7, July, 1954, Bureau of Business and Economic Research, State University of Iowa, Iowa City, Iowa . . . (Price on request.)*

67. SOCIAL SECURITY IN THE UNITED STATES. *U. S. Dept. of Health, Education, and Welfare, Social Security Administration, 1959. U. S. Government Printing Office, Washington 25, D. C. . . . 58pp. . . . 35¢*

68. TO MEET THE AMERICAN PEOPLE'S NEEDS. *Labor's Economic Review, Vol. 4, No. 6–7, July-July, 1959, AFL-CIO Dept. of Research, AFL-CIO Building, 815 Sixteenth Street, N.W., Washington 6, D. C. . . . 25¢*

69. INDIVIDUAL AND GROUP SECURITY. *A Study in Economic Principles and Human Well-Being, The American Competitive Enterprise Economy, No. XV, Chamber of Commerce of the United States, 1615 H Street, N.W., Washington, D. C., 1959 . . . 34pp. . . . 50¢*

D. International Economics

70. AMERICA AND THE WORLD ECONOMY. *Basic Economics, The Industrial Relations Center, The University of Chicago, Chicago 37, Illinois, 1954 . . . 34pp. . . . 50¢*

71. INTERNATIONAL ECONOMIC PROBLEMS. *Economic Series 2, by James D. Calderwood. Curriculum Resources, Inc., 1515 W. Lake Street, Minneapolis 8, Minn., 1961 . . . 70pp. . . . $1.00*

72. WORLD TRADE. *Economic Series 31, by James D. Calderwood and Hazel J. Jones. Curriculum Resources, Inc., 1515 W. Lake Street, Minneapolis 8, Minn., 1961 . . . 68pp. . . . 90¢*

73. UNITED STATES TARIFF POLICY. *A Statement on National Policy by the Research and Policy Committee of the Committee for Economic Development, 711 Fifth Ave., New York 22, N. Y., November, 1954 . . . 48pp. . . . (Out of print.)*

74. PETITION OF THE CANDLEMAKERS *by Frederic Bastiat, Outside Readings in Economics, Arleigh P. Hess, ed., Thomas Y. Crowell Company, 432 Park Avenue South, New York, N. Y., 1956 . . . 502pp. . . . $2.50 . . . (Excerpt in preparation, price on request.)*

75. NEW DIRECTIONS IN U. S. FOREIGN ECONOMIC POLICY *by Richard N. Gardner. Headline Series No. 133, Foreign Policy Association, Inc., 345 E. 46th Street, New York 17, N. Y., January-February, 1959 . . . 77pp. . . . 50¢*

76. FORGING A UNITED EUROPE, THE STORY OF THE EUROPEAN COMMUNITY *by Robert L. Heilbroner. Public Affairs Pamphlet No. 308, Public Affairs Committee, Inc., 22 East 38th Street, New York 16, N. Y., January, 1961 . . . 28pp. . . . 25¢*

E. Economic Growth in Advanced and Underdeveloped Nations

77. HIGH EMPLOYMENT AND GROWTH IN THE AMERICAN ECONOMY *by Herbert Stein and Edward F. Denison, Chapter 7, Goals For Americans. Prentice-Hall, Inc., Englewood Cliffs, N. J., 1960 . . . 372pp. . . . $1.00*

78. ECONOMIC GROWTH. *Chapter 8, from An Introduction to Economic Reasoning, by Marshall A. Robinson, Herbert C. Morton, and James D. Calderwood. The Brookings Institution, 1775 Massachusetts Avenue, N.W., Washington 6, D. C., 1959 . . . 335pp. . . . $3.00 . . . (Excerpt price . . . 50¢)*

79. THE AMERICAN ECONOMY: IS IT GROWING FAST ENOUGH? *Vital Issues, Vol. IX, No. 9, Center for Information on America, Washington, Conn., October, 1960 . . . 35¢*

80. THE CHALLENGE TO AMERICA: ITS ECONOMIC AND SOCIAL ASPECTS. *Special Studies Project Report IV, Rockefeller Brothers Fund, America at Mid-Century Series. Doubleday & Company, Inc., Garden City, New York, 1958 . . . 78pp. . . . 75¢*

81. ECONOMIC GROWTH IN THE UNITED STATES—ITS PAST AND FUTURE. *A Statement on National Policy by the Research and Policy Committee of the Committee for Economic Development, 711 Fifth Avenue, New York 22, N. Y., February, 1958 . . . 62pp. . . . 50¢*

82. THE PROMISE OF ECONOMIC GROWTH: PROSPECTS, COSTS, CONDITIONS. *Report of the Committee on Economic Policy, Chamber of Commerce of the United States, 1615 H Street, N.W., Washington 6, D. C., 1960 . . . 55pp. . . . $1.00*

83. UNDERDEVELOPED LANDS, "REVOLUTION OF RISING EXPECTATIONS" *by Forrest D. Murden. Headline Series, No. 119, Foreign Policy Association, 345 East 46th St., New York 17, N. Y., Sept.-Oct., 1956 . . . 62pp. . . . 50¢*

84. A DOOR TO THE PRESENT. *A discussion of current programs and problems of technical assistance, by James D. Calderwood and Laurence de Rycke, Monograph Series No. 1, International Development Placement Association, Inc., 345 East 46th Street, New York 17, N. Y., May, 1954 . . . 39pp. . . . (pp. 5–16) . . . (Out of print.)*

85. THE GROWING WORLD: ECONOMIC DEVELOPMENT AND THE WORLD BANK *by Robert L. Heilbroner, Public Affairs Pamphlet, No. 237, Public Affairs Pamphlets, 22 East 38th Street, New York 16, N. Y., July, 1956 . . . 28pp. . . . 25¢*

86. THE MUTUAL SECURITY PROGRAM, Fiscal Year 1961. *A Summary Presentation, Department of State, Department of Defense, International Cooperation Administration, Development Loan Fund. U. S. Government Printing Office, Washington 25, D. C., March, 1960 . . . 125pp. . . . 55¢*

F. Economic Systems

87. ECONOMIC SYSTEMS IN ACTION: THE UNITED STATES, THE SOVIET UNION, THE UNITED KINGDOM *by Alfred R. Oxenfeldt. Holt, Rinehart and Winston, Inc., 383 Madison Avenue, New York 17, N. Y., 1957 . . . 207pp. . . . $2.75*

88. AMERICAN CAPITALISM, AN INTRODUCTION FOR YOUNG CITIZENS. *CASE Economic Literacy Series No. 1, Council for Advancement of Secondary Education, 1201 Sixteenth Street, N.W., Washington 6, D. C., 1958 . . . 116pp. . . . $1.00*

89. METHODS OF ORGANIZING ECONOMIC ACTIVITY IN THE UNITED STATES AND THE SOVIET UNION *by Lewis E. Wagner, Economic Topics, 1960-61, Joint Council on Economic Education, 2 West 46 Street, New York 36, N. Y. . . . 8pp. . . . 10¢*

90. SOVIET ECONOMIC POWER, Its Organization, Growth and Challenge *by Robert W. Campbell. Houghton Mifflin Company, The Riverside Press, Cambridge, Mass., 1960 . . . 209pp. . . . $1.95 . . . (paper edition)*

G. Historical Approach to Economic Matters

91. THE BIG CHANGE: AMERICA TRANSFORMS ITSELF, 1900–1950 *by Frederick Lewis Allen, Bantam Books, 271 Madison Avenue, New York, N. Y., January, 1961 . . . 288pp. . . . 50¢*

92. AMERICAN CAPITALISM: ITS PROMISE AND ACCOMPLISHMENT *by Louis M. Hacker. An Anvil Original, D. Van Nostrand Company, Inc., 120 Alexander Street, Princeton, New Jersey, 1957 . . . 190pp. . . . $1.25*

93. BASIC HISTORY OF AMERICAN BUSINESS *by Thomas C. Cochran. An Anvil Original, D. Van Nostrand Company, Inc., 120 Alexander Street, Princeton, New Jersey, 1959 . . . 191pp. . . . $1.25*

94. THE AMERICAN FARMER IN A CHANGING WORLD *by Walter W. Wilcox;* AGRICULTURE'S TECHNOLOGICAL REVOLUTION *by Glenn L. Johnson. Excerpt from United States Agriculture: Perspectives and Prospects, The American Assembly, Graduate School of Business, Columbia University, New York 27, N. Y., May, 1955 . . . 31pp. . . . 50¢*

95. LABOR AND THE AMERICAN WAY *by Mark Starr. Oxford Social Studies Pamphlets, Oxford Book Company, 71 Fifth Avenue, New York 3, N. Y., 1960 . . . 92pp. . . . 65¢*

96. THE WORLDLY PHILOSOPHERS *by Robert L. Heilbroner. Simon & Schuster, Inc., 630 Fifth Avenue, New York, N. Y., 1961 . . . 309pp. . . . $1.50*

Suggested Methods for Teachers

chapter seven
Raymond H. Muessig
Vincent R. Rogers

> . . . The pressure of economic distress will teach men, if anything can, that realities are less dangerous than fancies, that fact-finding is more effective than fault-finding. . . .
>
> CARL BECKER

INTRODUCTION

To some extent, a parallel can be drawn between aspects of education and economics. Most people possess and express a degree of "conventional wisdom" regarding educational and economic matters. In the educational realm, for example, many laymen embrace a group of firm convictions based upon a cluster of readily accepted truisms with reference to what is "good," "bad," or "needed" if we are going to "run a tight ship." They may feel that a return to "old-fashioned discipline" is indicated; that the 3 R's have lost out to a host of "silly fads and frills"; and that rigid "pass-fail standards" should be maintained or reinstituted regardless of what may happen to the recipients of "F" grades. Irrespective of background, training, or experience, a number of Americans feel competent to judge, advise, criticize, and even abuse professionals engaged in the process of educating our youth. The classroom teacher's expertise is often thought of as "mere common sense" (unless, by some quirk of fate, the layman finds himself facing thirty to forty restless, squirming, enthusiastic, heterogeneous youngsters!).

Similarly, everyone has ideas and opinions about economics. A perusal of the letters-to-the-editor columns of most daily newspapers will reveal an interesting collection of "down-to-earth" exhortations. One letter may stress the "obvious fact" that just as a "responsible" family is able to operate within a firm, balanced budget so can and must the government. Another may demand that we "buy *American, only American.*" And still another statement may deplore governmental "meddling" in economic matters that are "best left alone" because they "naturally take care of themselves in time."

It might well be said that in both education and economics a little knowledge is worse than none. What is desperately needed in both fields is not a "little knowledge" but rather a substantial amount of understanding and sustained, sympathetic interest. The Great Depression of the thirties, among other calamities our nation and our world have experienced, illustrated dramatically the nature and significance of the crucial relationship existing between economic and political commitments. Only the most uninformed and callous among us can be completely unaware that one of the basic problems involved in living and surviving today is that of the haves and the have-nots, both here and abroad. The economic condition of an earlier day that was characterized by Western domination of world trade—frequently to the control or exclusion of other areas—has been altered. Non-western societies of the sixties refuse to be excluded or exploited; they, too, want a place in the sun.

Traditionally, economics has received only token attention in the history-geography dominated social studies curricula of our public schools. It now appears that economics will play a more prominent role at both the elementary and secondary levels — if current proposals, projects, and experimental programs are used as an indicator. In this chapter, we will not summarize, react to, or endorse any of the endeavors in which economists, social studies educators, teachers, and others are now engaged. Rather, we will attempt to sketch for the reader a variety of procedural possibilities adaptable to many existing courses of study. The approaches suggested in the pages that follow have been tailored to five generalizations drawn from the preceding chapters by Professors Martin and Miller.

1. Every Society Has Some Kind of Economic System. This Pattern of Arrangements Involves the Production, Distribution, and Use of Goods and Services and Reflects the Values and Objectives of the Particular Society.

Each society has its unique set of values and objectives and an economic system that stems from the things it prizes and seeks. While an economic system is an abstraction, it emerges out of very real human needs, wants, problems, aspirations, and commitments. Many scholars have recognized and dealt with the fascinating and important relationship that exists between *whys* of given cultures and resulting *who, what, when, where,* and *how* facets of economic behavior. The following statements by social scientists reveal a concern with this relationship:

> To the anthropologist economic relationships are part of an overall system of social relationships (however weakly this system be structured and integrated). The economic system (or sub-system) is therefore to be fully understood only in a context of social, political, ritual, moral and even aesthetic activities and values, and in turn affects these. . . .[1]

> The economic machinery of a society appears in quite a new light if it is studied in relation to the social structure. The exchange of goods and services is dependent upon, is the result of, and at the same time is a means of maintaining a certain structure, a network of relations between persons and collections of persons. . . . [2]

> . . . In understanding the nature of society it is essential to recognize that social institutions make up an integrated web of which the economic form a major part. And in understanding the nature of man it is essential to recognize that his motivations are all but determined by the web of social insitutions within which he operates. . . .[3]

> Since the economic state of a society is closely related to its political state, and the forces that bring change in the one also bring some sort of change in the other, a model that explains economic growth must take into account noneconomic as well as economic aspects of human behavior. . . .[4]

[1] Raymond Firth, "Capital, Saving and Credit in Peasant Societies: A Viewpoint from Economic Anthropology," Essay Number 1 in Raymond Firth and B. S. Yamey (eds.), *Capital, Saving and Credit in Peasant Societies* (Chicago: Aldine Publishing Co., 1964), p. 16.

[2] A. R. Radcliffe-Brown, *Structure and Function in Primitive Society* (New York: Free Press of Glencoe, Inc., 1952), pp. 197-198.

[3] Daniel B. Fusfeld, "Economic Theory Misplaced: Livelihood In Primitive Society," Essay Number XVII in Karl Polanyi, Conrad M. Arensberg, and Harry W. Pearson (eds.), *Trade and Market in the Early Empires: Economies in History and Theory* (New York: Free Press of Glencoe, Inc., 1957), p. 343.

[4] Everett E. Hagen, *On the Theory of Social Change: How Economic Growth Begins* (Homewood, Illinois: The Dorsey Press, Inc., 1962), p. 25.

There are numerous procedures teachers might employ to help
children and youth develop an awareness of the presence of an economic
system in their own society and others as well as some understanding
and feeling for certain of the links that join societal values and economic
systems. Depending on the developmental stages, backgrounds, interests,
and abilities of young people in their classes, teachers could use approaches ranging from the most simple, basic exposure to a more
thorough study in some depth. With pupils in the upper primary and the
intermediate grades, for example, the teacher might launch a series of
articulated and expansive learning experiences centered on this first
economic generalization by inviting children to identify, share, and discuss their hobbies and the things they collect and trade. Class members
might be interested in such things as sports and monster picture cards
packaged with bubble gum, buttons and pins, flags and pennants,
license plates, marbles, bottle caps, rocks, shells, stamps, coins, etc.
Gradually, the teacher could focus class discussion on one or two of the
items most popular with his charges. Assuming, for instance, that a
group of the boys gathered and exchanged baseball picture cards, the
teacher could ask a series of questions similar to these:

Why do you collect these cards?
How much do you pay for a package of cards? About how much is the
   bubble gum in the package worth? Then, about how much are you
   paying for each of the cards?
Do you ever get the same pictures when you buy more packages of cards?
   If you do, what do you do with pictures that are alike? Are these
   same pictures worth as much to you as different ones? Why or why not?
When you trade cards, do you always trade one card for one card? Or,
   are there times when you trade two or more of your cards for one card
   another boy has or one of your cards for two or more cards another boy
   has? When you are trading, how do you know how much a card is
   worth?
If you have all of the cards for one baseball team are they worth any
   more as a set? Why or why not?
If you ever got all of the cards made by the company that sells them what
   might you do? Why?

By helping his entire class review the boys' responses to the
questions above, the teacher should be able to move pupils easily and
naturally into a meaningful analysis of the *values* and the *economic
system* implicit in what has been said. With **assistance, the children**

should be able to see that the boys who collect baseball picture cards do so for various, but identifiable, reasons. Other boys in the class and in different locales and certainly many girls in and out of the class have little or no knowledge of the cards or desire to gather them; they seek different objects. For the boys who do prize the cards, however, these snapshots may be either *bartered* or *purchased* with some form of accepted *currency*. Many boys regard duplicate cards as a *surplus commodity* that can be traded for a medium of exchange.

There is a dimension of the "card-trading economic system" originated and perfected by collectors in this kind of situation which would probably emerge and which should be interesting and revealing to the class. While the unit price of each picture is the same at the time of purchase, some cards are regarded as being or becoming more valuable than others for purposes of exchange. A miniature *supply and demand* phenomenon develops. For example, the photograph of a famous star might be traded for several pictures of less-famous athletes. Yet the more scarce snapshots of lesser players whose pictures are "needed" to complete a set may be exchanged for "more cards than they are *really* worth."

Occasionally, a *monetary* system may be temporarily substituted for bartering. This occurs when a boy who wants a particular card does not have a picture to trade that another boy needs and therefore pays money for a single photograph.

Some of the economic terms and concepts we have used in this illustration could be used by the teacher and the children in some instances, but they are not of prime importance. The key point here is the relationship between values and an economic system, and we believe that youngsters could move toward this important idea as a result of the type of procedure sketched here.

⋁ Senior high school students might be exposed to social and political values with economic connotations and overtones through the use of a problem situation followed by a group of interviews in their community. The classroom teacher could launch this project by giving each of his students five mimeographed copies of a case such as this one:

> Orchardville is a suburban community with approximately 12,000 residents. It is next to Adamstown, a city which has a population of close to 300,000. Many of the skilled laborers, technicians, businessmen, and professionals who live in Orchardville work in Adamstown. Orchardville has a fairly small business and professional district and a rather large village-style shopping center. It has no industry. The residents hope to

keep it that way, though they do complain at times about their high taxes. They like their clean, quiet community with its lovely trees, beautiful lawns, flowers, and shrubs, attractive park, wide streets, and nice homes. Orchardville is proud of its schools: one senior high school, two junior high schools, and six elementary schools. Its cultural facilities include a rather small public library, contributed 25 years ago by a wealthy industrialist in Adamstown; the high school auditorium, used for lectures and for some amateur dramatic and musical programs; and a bandstand in the park. Orchardville's recreational facilities include baseball fields at all of the schools; tennis courts at the high school and the park; a public ice skating rink; a private country club with a golf course; and a commercial bowling alley.

Orchardville has no swimming pool, however, and that is where the problem arises. Everyone who wants to swim must drive into Adamstown. Parents who desire swimming lessons for their children find this especially inconvenient. While a number of Orchardville residents see the need for a pool, there seems to be rather strong disagreement as to how this project should be handled financially. The following are some of the suggestions that have been made and certain problems associated with these proposals:

1. The pool should be built at the local high school and paid for out of district funds. It might be an indoor-outdoor pool. Throughout the regular school year it would be used for instruction during the day and family recreation several nights a week. It would operate as a public pool all summer long. Admission might or might not be charged evenings and summers. A special school bond levy would have to be passed under this system, for the schools already need all monies currently available to them.

2. Municipal funds should be used to construct the pool. The use of the pool could be free to all residents of Orchardville, however, only if the voters would approve an additional tax assessment.

3. The pool should be built with municipal funds secured through the sale of bonds. Admission would have to be charged so the bonds could be paid off.

4. Funds from the state or national government should be obtained for the construction of the pool or some kind of matching funds arrangement worked out. It is not known whether such funds could be secured or whether certain conditions might be attached to this system.

5. Contributions should be secured from public-minded people for the building of the pool. Many local citizens would have to volunteer to solicit funds from the residents of Orchardville. It might not be possible to secure enough money for a pool in this manner, or it could be a very slow process.

6. The pool should be constructed by an individual or a company as a private business venture. Admission would have to be charged, of course. This might not be a profitable enterprise.

7. Etc.

How do you think this project should be handled? Why do you believe this is the best way to go about it? Do you see any problems in your plan?

Are there other approaches you would accept? Which ones? Why?

Are there some ways of carrying out a pool construction program that you would not accept? Which ones? Why?

On the back of the first of the five copies of this problem situation each student would write his own responses to the questions asked at the close of the case statement. Class members would then share and discuss their feelings and systems of implementation. After reviewing interviewing procedures, the teacher would next request that every class member try to conduct four interviews. Each student might try to interview a friend, a younger married person, one of his parents, and a senior citizen to obtain some variety. After completing the interviews, students would read aloud in class selected comments of their interviewees. No effort would be made to tabulate, collate, or summarize responses, as the procedure could not presume to uncover "scientific" findings. Rather, emphasis would be on the interesting variety of values and systems suggested by the respondents.

Independent student research is a third way of getting at our generalization dealing with values and their economic implications and manifestations. Prior to initiating this activity "officially," the teacher should be the epitome of resourcefulness. Enlisting the aid of his senior high school students, their parents, his friends and professional colleagues, librarians, people in used bookstores, etc., he should try to stock his room with an abundance of old and new materials pertaining to the American economic picture. These resources might include newspaper stories and editorials; articles in periodicals; transcripts of speeches; printed creeds, position statements, and platforms of individuals, groups, organizations, and political parties; published reports of persons and agencies; diaries; letters; pamphlets; booklets; books. After identifying items for their return to lenders, a student committee could create its own topical catalog. Materials could be filed according to values, social philosophies, theories, themes, problems, periods, movements, and systems or by some other group of headings.

After sorting the resources, the teacher might help each student find an area of independent investigation suited to that individual's interests and abilities. Every student would then read selections tailored to his topic and his capacities. For example, a student interested in various individuals' economic values and their possible consequences would encounter many telling statements such as the ones excerpted below. The first passage is from Andrew Carnegie's essay, "Wealth," written in 1889. The second is part of a radio address by John D. Rockefeller, Jr. in 1941. And the third is from the presidential paper read to the American Economic Association by Theodore W. Schultz, Professor of Economics at the University of Chicago, in 1960.

. . . while the law [of competition] may be sometimes hard for the individual, it is best for the race, because it insures the survival of the fittest in every department. . . .

. . . .

. . . Neither the individual nor the race is improved by alms-giving. Those worthy of assistance, except in rare cases, seldom require assistance. The really valuable men of the race never do, except in cases of accident or sudden change. . . .⁵

———————

I believe in the supreme worth of the individual and in his right to life, liberty and the pursuit of happiness.

I believe that every right implies a responsibility; every opportunity, an obligation; every possession, a duty

I believe that the law was made for man and not man for the law; that government is the servant of the people and not their master.

I believe in the dignity of labor, whether with head or hand; that the world owes no man a living but that it owes every man an opportunity to make a living.

I believe that thrift is essential to well ordered living and that economy is a prime requisite of a sound financial structure, whether in government, business or personal affairs.⁶

———————

Although it is obvious that people acquire useful skills and knowledge, it is not obvious that these skills and knowledge are a form of capital, that this capital is in substantial part a product of deliberate

⁵ Andrew Carnegie, "Wealth," in Richard D. Heffner (ed.), *A Documentary History of the United States* (New York: New American Library of World Literature, Inc., 1956), pp. 168 and 172.
⁶ John D. Rockefeller, Jr., "Our Family Creed," in Lewis Copeland and Lawrence Lamm (eds.), *The World's Great Speeches* (New York: Dover Publications, Inc., 1958), p. 735.

investment, that it has grown in Western societies at a much faster rate than conventional (nonhuman) capital, and that its growth may well be the most distinctive feature of the economic system. . . .

Much of what we call consumption constitutes investment in human capital. Direct expenditures on education, health, and internal migration to take advantage of better job opportunities are clear examples. . . .

Economists have long known that people are an important part of the wealth of nations. Measured by what labor contributes to output, the productive capacity of human beings is now vastly larger than all other forms of wealth taken together. . . .

. . . By investing in themselves, people can enlarge the range of choice available to them. It is one way free men can enhance their welfare.[7]

A class member investigating economic aims and proposals of organizations might uncover a number of platforms such as the two abridged here for illustrative purposes. The first excerpt is from a position statement developed by the National Association of Manufacturers in 1904; the second, part of the 1918 "Economic Platform" of the American Federation of Labor.

1. Fair dealing is the fundamental and basic principle on which relations between employes and employers should rest.

. . . .

4. With due regard to contracts, it is the right of the employe to leave his employment whenever he sees fit, and it is the right of the employer to discharge any employe when he sees fit.

. . . .

6. Employers must be unmolested and unhampered in the management of their business, in determining the amount and quality of their product, and in the use of any methods or systems of pay which are just and equitable.[8]

ECONOMIC PLATFORM

1. The abolition of all forms of involuntary servitude, except as punishment for crime.

---

[7] Theodore W. Schultz, "Investment in Human Capital," in Edmund S. Phelps (ed.), *The Goal of Economic Growth* (New York: W. W. Norton & Company, Inc., 1962), pp. 106–107.

[8] "Proceedings of the Ninth Annual Convention of the National Association of Manufacturers of the United States of America held at Pittsburgh, Pa., May 17, 18, and 19, 1904," in Felix Flugel and Harold U. Faulkner (eds.), *Readings in the Economic and Social History of the United States* (New York: Harper & Row, Publishers, 1929), p. 808.

  2. Free schools, free textbooks and compulsory education.

. . . .

  4. A work day of not more than eight hours in the twenty-four hour day.

. . . .

  6. Release from employment one day in seven.

. . . .

  8. The municipal ownership of public utilities.
  9. The abolition of the sweat-shop system.

. . . .

  13. The passage of anti-child labor laws in states where they do not exist and rigid defense of them where they have been enacted into law.

. . . .

  19. We favor a system of finance whereby money shall be issued exclusively by the Government, with such regulations and restrictions as will protect it from manipulation by the banking interests for their own private gain.[9]

A senior high school student looking into the economic philosophy of our government as perceived, articulated, and carried out by its chief executive could turn to presidential reports as a rich source of data. He should gain many insights from his reading and consideration of passages such as these, taken from President Johnson's Economic Report to the Congress of the United States, dated January 28, 1965:

> . . . Our goals for individuals and our Nation extend far beyond mere affluence. The quality of American life remains a constant concern.
> The task of economic policy is to create a prosperous America. *The unfinished task of prosperous Americans is to build a Great Society.*
> Our accomplishments have been many; these tasks remain unfinished:
> —to achieve full employment without inflation;
> —to restore external equilibrium and defend the dollar;
> —to enhance the efficiency and flexibility of our private and public economies;
> —to widen the benefits of prosperity;
> —to improve the quality of American life.

. . . .

> The 1966 Budget Message outlines my fiscal philosophy. We have four priorities:
> —to strengthen our national defense;
> —to meet our pressing human needs;

---

[9] In Flugel and Faulkner (eds.), *Readings in the Economic and Social History of the United States*, pp. 802–803.

> —to maximize the efficiency of Government operations;
> —to sustain the advance of our Nation's economy.
>
> . . . .
>
> *Through helping to raise incomes in less developed countries:* U. S. foreign assistance programs further three basic American aims. By helping to advance the economic growth of the less developed nations, they
>> —create the kind of world in which peace and freedom are most likely to flourish;
>> —bring closer a world economic order in which all nations will be strong partners;
>> —simultaneously, give a major stimulus to U.S. exports both in the present through direct financing of U.S. goods and services and for the future by developing the recipient's ability to buy and his preference for American products.
>
> . . . .
>
> . . . . No longer will we tolerate widespread involuntary idleness, unnecessary human hardship and misery, the impoverishment of whole areas, the spoiling of our natural heritage, the human and physical ugliness of our cities, the ravages of the business cycle, or the arbitrary redistribution of purchasing power through inflation.
>
> . . . .
>
> Our tools of economic policy are much better tools than existed a generation ago. We are able to proceed with much greater confidence and flexibility in seeking effective answers to the changing problems of our changing economy.[10]

In time, class members could prepare oral or written reports digesting findings and including interpretations and reactions. While detail, precision, and sophistication would probably be lacking in most student reports this first time, the crucial idea that values and economic systems are allied should come to the surface frequently. When students present or record unusually telling examples germane to the economic generalization being sought. the teacher could call the attention of the class to these illustrations and invite discussion.

A final technique which might be tried as a means of confronting senior high school students with our first basic economic observation has a definite anthropological orientation. As with the previous suggestion, the teacher could begin by stocking the shelves of his room library with

---

[10] In *Economic Report of the President: Together with the Annual Report of the Council of Economic Advisers* (Washington, D. C.: United States Government Printing Office, 1965), pp. 8, 9, 14, 20–21, and 21 respectively.

a number of appropriate sources, varied in their content and level of difficulty. The following are some works which might be obtained:

Ruth Benedict, *Patterns of Culture* (New York: New American Library of World Literature, Inc., 1934).

Raymond Firth and B. S. Yamey (eds.), *Capital, Saving and Credit in Peasant Societies* (Chicago: Aldine Publishing Co., 1964).

Morton H. Fried (ed.), *Readings in Anthropology,* Vol. II (New York: Thomas Y. Crowell Company, 1959).

Walter Goldschmidt, *Man's Way* (New York: Holt, Rinehart and Winston, Inc., 1959).

——————————, *Ways of Mankind* (Boston: The Beacon Press, 1954).

Edward T. Hall, *The Silent Language* (Greenwich, Connecticut: Fawcett Publications, Inc., 1959).

Hugo Huber, *The Krobo: Traditional Social and Religious Life of a West African People. Studia Instituti Anthropos,* Vol. XVI (St. Augustin Near Bonn: The Anthropos Institute, 1963).

Godfrey Lienhardt, *Social Anthropology* ("Home University Library" [London: Oxford University Press, 1964]).

Ralph Linton, *The Tree of Culture* (New York: Alfred A. Knopf, Inc., 1955).

Margaret Mead (ed.), *Cultural Patterns and Technical Change* (New York: New American Library of World Literature, Inc., 1955).

Karl Polanyi, Conrad M. Arensberg, and Harry W. Pearson (eds.), *Trade and Market in the Early Empires: Economies in History and Theory* (New York: Free Press of Glencoe, Inc., 1957).

A. R. Radcliffe-Brown, *Structure and Function in Primitive Society* (New York: Free Press of Glencoe, Inc., 1952).

Audrey I. Richards, *Hunger and Work in a Savage Tribe: A Functional Study of Nutrition Among the Southern Bantu* (Cleveland, Ohio: The World Publishing Company, 1964). First published by George Routledge & Sons, Ltd., in 1932.

Elman R. Service, *Primitive Social Organization: An Evolutionary Perspective* (New York: Random House, Inc., 1962).

William N. Stephens, *The Family in Cross-cultural Perspective* (New York: Holt, Rinehart and Winston, Inc., 1963).

As an alternative to the independent research approach outlined in the preceding illustration, the teacher might employ a committee system for this project. If he has a highly heterogeneous class, he may want to put a student who reads well and another who writes clearly into each small group, since these are necessary skills for the kind of endeavor conceived here. Committees could be arranged in a number of ways. Each committee might be assigned to a book, asked to find salient passages, and digest and paraphrase material in its own words. Or, each small group might specialize in the values and economic system of a particular culture such as the Blackfoot, the Navaho, the Reindeer Chukchee, the Bantu, the Krobo, or others. A third possibility would be for a committee to select a single economic concept such as the market, interdependence, division of labor, medium of exchange, or interest, and to search for cultures in which the concept might be applied to patterns of behavior.

The teacher who arranges his committees the third way might introduce his students to the project by reading aloud sections from anthropological works which identify a few of the over-all values of a group of cultures. He might read slowly, pausing for students' questions or comments. His purpose here is to set the stage for committee work by sensitizing his class to values as seen from a cross-cultural perspective. While there would be economic overtones in some of the selections, he would not underline them at this point. Excerpts such as these might serve the intended purpose:

> Health and strength are perhaps the best of the good things of life for the Navaho. If you aren't healthy, you can't work; if you don't work, you'll starve. Industry is enormously valued. A family must arise and be about their tasks early, for if someone goes by and sees no smoke drifting out of the smokehole it will be thought that "there is something wrong there; somebody must be sick." In enumerating the virtues of a respected man or woman the faithful performance of duties is always given a prominent place. "If you are poor or a beggar, people will make fun of you. If you are lazy people will make fun of you."
>
> By Navaho standards one is industrious in order to accumulate possessions—within certain limits—and to care for the possessions he obtains. Uncontrolled gambling or drinking are disapproved primarily because they are wasteful. The "good" man is one who has "hard goods" (turquoise and jewelry mainly), "soft goods" (clothing, etc.), "flexible goods" (textiles, etc.), and songs, stories, and other intangible property, of which ceremonial knowledge is the most important. An old Navaho said to W. W. Hill, "I have always been a poor man. I do not know a single song." The final disrespect is to say of a man, "Why, he hasn't even a dog."
>
> A good appearance is valued; while this is partly a matter of physique, figure, and facial appearance, it means even more the ability

to dress well and to appear with a handsome horse and substantial trappings.

. . . .

Personal excellence is thus a value, but personal "success" in the white American sense is not. The Navaho lack of stress upon the success goal has its basis in childhood training but is reinforced by various patterns of adult life. A white man may start out to make a fortune and continue piling it up until he is a millionaire, where a Navaho, though also interested in accumulating possessions, will stop when he is comfortably off, or even sooner, partly for fear of being called a witch if he is too successful. . . .[11]

When the Blackfoot Indians were taught farming and given farm equipment by the Canadian government, the project was a dismal failure, for it required types of activity that ran contrary to Blackfoot values: sedentary life, a hard daily routine, emphasis on the separateness of the individual household, and husbanding of resources rather than a pattern of general sharing and generosity. When cattle were introduced, however, the Blackfoot elite took to the new symbol which so closely resembled the keeping of horses, which had been the former chief value symbol.[12]

We have to realize, in fact, that the *secondary* values centered round cattle among the South-Eastern Bantu come to predominate over the *primary*. The herd is less important as a source of meat, milk, and leather, than as the object of social ambitions, rivalries and emotions. Cattle become an attribute of leadership, a means of expressing ties of relationship, and a centre of religious life. At birth a man becomes a member of a group which is intimately associated with the herd of beasts which it owns; throughout life his obligations to his fellow-tribesmen are largely carried out by the exchange of heads of stock: at death this is the chief form of inheritance he leaves. The people are therefore more passionately attached to cattle, than to any other possession, even though they are more dependent on their fields for support.[13]

---

[11] Clyde Kluckhohn, "The Philosophy of the Navaho Indians," in Morton H. Fried (ed.), *Readings in Anthropology*, Vol. II (New York: Thomas Y. Crowell Company, 1959), pp. 441–443.
[12] Walter Goldschmidt, *Man's Way* (New York: Holt, Rinehart and Winston, Inc., 1959), p. 79.
[13] Audrey I. Richards, *Hunger and Work in a Savage Tribe: A Functional Study of Nutrition Among the Southern Bantu* (Cleveland, Ohio: The World Publishing Company, 1964), p. 97. First published by George Routledge & Sons, Ltd., in 1932. World publishing rights granted by Routledge & Kegan Paul Ltd.

The practical necessity in some societies to relieve the wants of others, may further be recognized as a binding religious duty. So the *zakat*, or legal alms, which are demanded of Moslems, rank in religious importance with prayer and fasting; what is due in alms-giving is doctrinally defined. Whatever the practice, the *rule* is that one-fifth of the value of buried treasure, for example, or the value of metals taken from mines, must be given to the needy. Religious prescription has here an economic function.[14]

Having constructed a value-oriented foundation, the teacher could establish committees and move from group to group, providing materials and suggestions. He should emphasize several times the caveat that student committees built around Western-American economic concepts will be looking through their own lenses at values and economic systems in other cultures. This view may facilitate study and communication, but it can distort percepts of other peoples who do not operate within the same conceptual framework.

In its explorations, the Market Committee should come upon items such as this:

A typical cause for confusion, distrust, and hostility arising out of a difference in the system of categories is the fact that Navahos are today dependent upon a distant and mysterious white institution called "the market." In the days of bartering raw materials, a sheep or a sack of wool maintained a rather constant value. At present, when both are sold to the trader, the Navaho never know in advance whether the lamb will bring ten cents a pound or only five cents, and they see no sense in these variations. They share the common distrust of farmer folk for those who buy and resell the products of their hard labors, but they are at a greater disadvantage than the white farmer because they are unfamiliar with white marketing customs and have no means of understanding the reasons for the apparently senseless fluctuations in price and demand. Moreover, since they feel that they usually are underpaid for their sheep and wool and that the price they will get varies with no rhyme or reason, they feel uncertain about improving their products. Why should they invest money, labor, and time simply to benefit the trader or the more remote livestock dealers? Similar confusion and irritation resulted from the government's program of killing "excess" livestock. From the Navaho point of view only production is ethical. Destruction—except to satisfy immediate hunger—is unethical.[15]

---

[14] Godfrey Lienhardt, *Social Anthropology* ("Home University Library"[London: Oxford University Press, 1964]), p. 96.

[15] Kluckhohn, *op. cit.*, pp. 445–446.

The committee concerned with interdependence might find excerpts such as the following:

. . . [The] Melanesians had developed complex patterns of local specialization in which a particular tribe produced one or two things in quantity and traded their products over a wide area. This was the more surprising since every Melanesian tribe was constantly at war with at least some of its neighbors. The result was a curious pattern of economic interdependence and social avoidance.

The tribal specialization often involved the commonest and most necessary tools and utensils. Thus in the Admiralty Islands one tribe made all the matting mosquito bags used in the group, another produced most of the pottery. An interior tribe in one island made all the nets used by the coast tribes for fishing. Still another tribe produced all the weapons used in the group. This specialization probably developed because it was the only tribe which had in its territory obsidian for making dagger blades and spearheads. Even tribes which were at war with the weapon makers relied on them for armament, obtaining their munitions at second or third hand through neutrals.[16]

Cross-cultural insights into division of labor could be supported by material discovered by this committee. This group might report that

Among the Reindeer Chukchee, women work much harder than men, especially the younger ones. The man's part of the work is the herding, catching, and slaughtering of the animals, the hunt, carrying of heavy logs and of the stones necessary to hold the tent firmly in place; also work on wood with axe, hatchet, and knife, and so forth. The harnessing of the reindeer is done by both sexes, also carrying fuel from the bush, and chopping wood and ice. The loading and unloading of sledges is performed for the most part by women. The care of the house, which in the nomadic life of an arctic climate requires almost uninterrupted toil, falls wholly to the share of the women, also skinning and butchering, gathering roots, preparing food, dressing skins, making garments, and much more, not to speak of the duties of the mother. Moreover, man almost never shares in the woman's part of the work; he does not even know how it is performed. . . .[17]

The Medium of Exchange Committee could uncover examples of values and economic systems in a number of settings.

[16] Ralph Linton, *The Tree of Culture* (New York: Alfred A. Knopf, Inc., 1955), pp. 195–196.
[17] William N. Stephens, *The Family in Cross-Cultural Perspective* (New York: Holt, Rinehart and Winston, Inc., 1963), pp. 279–280.

Most Melanesian societies were wealth-obsessed. While, in Polynesia, the proper technique for exchange of property was that of voluntary gift and return of carefully balanced value, Melanesian economics seem a parody of modern finance. There were stone, dog tooth, feather, mat, and a numerous variety of shell currencies in different parts of the area. Sometimes half a dozen currencies would be in use in a single locality, with fluctuating exchange rates. Moreover, only certain currencies could be used for particular transactions, such as dowry or land purchase. . . .[18]

Among the Tapirapé wealth is not reckoned in terms of basic subsistence, for these goods are so easy to obtain as to be considered with little regard. The possessions that lend real distinction of wealth are such luxury articles as the breast and tail feathers of the red parrot. . ., beads, and pieces of hardware acquired through contact with white men or trading with other Indians. These goods are accordingly the most valued media of exchange in the community. Other goods used for a medium of exchange were . . . tobacco, extra hammocks, decorated gourds, string for binding feathers to arrows, and cane arrow shafts.[19]

And, the group specializing in interest might locate illustrations such as this:

A common form of investment is in lending paddy (unhusked rice). The cultivation of paddy in this district begins in mid-June and the first harvest appears about the third week in September. The main harvest is reaped in the first two weeks of December. The price of paddy is lowest after the main harvest but from February until about October it rises steadily as more and more people exhaust their stock and are forced to buy or borrow. The demand is intensified in August and again during the harvest months, since it is the practice sometimes to pay labourers in paddy or cooked food. Paddy (being grain in the husk) will last, so I was told, for four years if properly stored. Those who have a surplus lend paddy between February and October, and get it back after the December harvest at 50 per cent interest. Seed paddy (paddy grown the previous year) commands 100 per cent interest.[20]

---

[18] Linton, *op. cit.*, p. 196.

[19] Charles Wagley, "Tapirapé Shamanism," in Fried (ed.), *Readings in Anthropology*, Vol. II, pp. 406–407.

[20] F. G. Bailey, "Capital Saving and Credit in Highland Orissa (India)," Essay Number 6 in Firth and Yamey (eds.), *Capital, Saving and Credit in Peasant Societies*, p. 112.

As soon as the individual committee reports have been turned in, the teacher might ask his class to nominate students for an editing committee. The Editing Committee could work on a class publication entitled "Values and Economic Systems in Many Cultures" and each student could be given a copy. Other class activities, based on this paper, might emerge naturally and give students even more of a grasp of this first economic generalization.

2. All Economic Systems Are Confronted by the Problem of Relative Scarcity, of Unlimited Wants and Limited Resources.

James Tobin, Sterling Professor of Economics at Yale University and a member of the Council of Economic Advisers under President Kennedy, has written that "The allocation of resources among competing uses is *the* central and classical theoretical problem of economics." [21] Frank H. Knight once observed, "Each wants to have more of anything, little matter what, of which there is not enough to satisfy everyone." [22]

Man *does* seem to have unlimited wants which are expressed and sought in myriad ways. His desires range from the "here-and-now" to the "someday," from the "practical" to the "impractical," and from the "ridiculous" to the "sublime." He will probably *never* satisfy all of his acquired, secondary needs, for new wants are constantly taking shape. The "necessities" for the American of 1850, for example, have been vastly expanded for his modern counterpart to include indoor plumbing, central heating, an automatic washing machine, a television set, an automobile, an education for his children, and on and on. Whatever man *perceives* as "essential" may become essential in fact, regardless of an item's relative importance in terms of physical survival. Having mastered his primary needs, man is *still* subject to a host of other desires. As John Kenneth Galbraith put it, "when man has satisfied his physical needs, then psychologically grounded desires take over. These can never be satisfied. . . ." [23]

---

[21] "Growth Through Taxation," in Edmund S. Phelps (ed.), *The Goal of Economic Growth* (New York: W. W. Norton & Company, Inc., 1962), p. 88.

[22] "Free Society: Its Basic Nature and Problem," in Frank H. Knight, *On the History and Method of Economics: Selected Essays* (Chicago: Phoenix Books, The University of Chicago Press, 1963), p. 297.

[23] *The Affluent Society* (Boston: Houghton Mifflin Company, 1958), p. 143.

The advertising industry is largely devoted to the 'creation and perpetuation of a staggering variety of wants and desires, most of which are anything but "basic" to physical survival. If people *were* content merely to survive, however, there might be little need for a science of economics or for economists to study and advance it. Similarly, if all the world's inhabitants had *everything* their hearts desired; if all goods and services were free; and if the problem of unlimited wants and limited resources did not exist, economics and economists could become the superfluous appendages of a bygone era. But the fact remains that man's wants are boundless and his resources proscribed. This is the key issue of any economic system.

Man must choose from possible and plausible alternatives. He must ask and seek answers to questions such as: What goods and services are wanted, and why are they desired? What is the relationship between the demand for these goods and services and their supply? How can and should these goods be produced and these services provided? By whom should particular functions be performed? Even the wealthiest country must decide how it will utilize its available natural and human resources. A horn of plenty still has sides and a bottom. Although a society may operate well above a subsistence level, it must continually weigh goals, decide which routes it will travel, and deliberate about consequences of the journeys it has made.

Primary children might begin to explore our second generalization from economics—dealing with unlimited wants and limited resources— through a discussion of real and/or hypothetical vacation plans. Nine or ten weeks prior to the close of the school year the teacher could write travel agencies and other sources at home and abroad, requesting materials designed to stimulate interest in other places. Then, two or three weeks before the summer vacation period, the teacher could place pictures and posters around the classroom and circulate and read from descriptive brochures. The children could be encouraged to consider possibilities ranging from camping to a stay at a luxurious resort hotel; from a boat trip to Avalon to a ride on a ski lift in Switzerland; from Disneyland to Colonial Williamsburg; from Denmark's famous Tivoli amusement park to the Eiffel Tower. Next, each child would be given a chance to share with the class his list of imaginary vacation preferences. At this point, however, the teacher could introduce two limitations: (1) the summer is only so long, and (2) the child's family would have only enough money to visit one place. The teacher would then ask every class member to identify *the* choice he would make and to give his reasons.

Depending on human relations factors present and the socio-economic level of the group, the teacher might then invite pupils to talk about their *real* summer vacation plans. One child may comment that his family will stay at home this year because it wants to take a big trip next year. Another youngster may say that his family will go to see his grandparents in Indiana *instead* of his grandparents in Pennsylvania this year in the hope that a Pennsylvania trip may be possible next year. Still another may say that his family cannot decide whether to go camping at Yellowstone *or* to visit Disneyland, and so on. In each case the point should be clear that *choices* necessarily reflect what a family most wants to do, what it can afford, and what it has time to do.

Similarly, children at most grade levels in the elementary school could deal with the same understanding through analysis of the possible uses for a fictitious weekly pay check. The teacher could use a flannel board as a means of visualizing and vivifying the elements involved and an informal story format to attract interest and hold attention. In preparation for this activity, the children could be asked to draw, cut out of magazines, and mount illustrations. The first picture placed on the flannel board would be that of a man identified as *Mr. Green.* On Friday afternoon after work, Mr. Green receives his weekly salary *check* for $150. This would be the second item to appear on the flannel board. On Saturday morning, Mr. Green goes to his neighborhood *bank* (a bank building is the third picture) to cash his check. He receives *30 five-dollar bills* (play money which the teacher has had mimeographed and has had the children cut into separate bills and which has been lined up on the flannel board as the fourth stage in the sequence). The Greens have borrowed money from the bank to buy a *house* (the fifth illustration is of a home). Mr. Green takes $30 of the money to make his mortgage payment at the end of the month. At this point, a member of the class could be asked by the teacher to come up to the flannel board and to remove the picture of the house and six of the five-dollar bills. This is money that cannot be spent for other purposes. The Greens have also borrowed money from the bank to buy a *car* (an automobile is the sixth cut-out). Mr. Green takes $20 from his weekly salary to put aside for this payment at the end of the month. A second child would detach the car and four bills. Mr. Green decides to deposit $15 in the family *savings account* (an illustration of a savings pass book) and $5 in the *Christmas*

Club (a picture of Santa Claus) to be used for gifts next December. Again, a third and a fourth child could walk to the front of the room and take the savings pass book and three bills and the Santa Claus picture and one bill from the flannel board. When Mr. Green gets home from the bank, he gives *Mrs. Green* (a cut-out of a mother) $25 for *groceries* (a photograph of a supermarket) and $10 to pay the *electricity bill* (drawing of an electric light bulb). Two more children pull off the grocery and electricity mountings and five and two bills respectively. After Mrs. Green returns from shopping at the supermarket in the early afternoon, she and Mr. Green ask their *children* (a picture of a boy and girl is pressed upon the flannel board) to decide whether they would prefer to go to a restaurant for hamburgers, french fries, and milkshakes for dinner or to eat left-overs at home and attend a drive-in movie. The teacher could pause at this stage and hold up cut-outs of an eating place and an outdoor theater and ask the class which choice they would make if they were the Green children. The class could be told that either of the treats, the restaurant meal or the price of admission to the theater and bags of popcorn, would cost $5. Assuming that the class elects the show, a picture of an *outdoor theater* could be displayed just long enough for another pupil to whisk it away with an accompanying five-dollar bill. On Sunday, the Greens attend *church* (a drawing of a church is placed on the flannel board). They make their usual $5 contribution for church and Sunday school. And, the church cut-out and a single bill are detached simultaneously.

Now, the class could be asked how much money the Green family has left out of its weekly pay check. The children would count the remaining bills and arrive at a figure of $35. The teacher would then bring out a string long enough to reach across the entire width of the classroom. The string could be tacked on each side of the room so it would be just above the heads of the children. On this string pupils would fasten a host of illustrations depicting other items for which the Greens might spend the remaining $35. They might make a down payment on a portable television set for their family room, *or* a piano so the children could begin taking lessons, *or* a vacation camping trailer, etc. They could buy a small record player for the children, *or* a complete table tennis set, *or* new outfits for the boy and girl, etc.

Through this approach, the class should discover easily the idea of unlimited wants and limited resources. The Green family will always have many things for which it can spend its income. But it will also have a budget within which it must operate.

Another approach which might prove fruitful for junior and senior high school students involves the use of material obtained from current newspapers and news magazines. The teacher would divide a portion of one of the classroom bulletin boards into three sections: "Local," "State," and "National." Under each heading he would place headlines and/or articles related to decision-making situations brought about by a relative scarcity condition. For example, under "Local" he might post an item about a business that decided to enlarge its plant in the immediate community rather than start a new branch operation in another city. In the "State" section he could tack a report describing the decision made by a railroad serving much of the state to eliminate seldom used stops so the resulting savings could be channeled into better equipment to improve service. The "National" column might include a story about the reduction of U.S. foreign aid to one country while, simultaneously, assistance is increased for another nation. Following a class discussion of all of the materials on the bulletin board, the teacher might invite students to continue to search for and to post additional examples of economic choices necessitated by limited resources. ✔

As students gain increased interest and insight into the use of contemporary materials to examine resource limitations, perhaps a column could be added to the bulletin board that would include some illustrations of the problems *individuals* have encountered in making similarly related decisions. Some senior high school teachers might also want to focus the attention of class members on this major economic idea through the role-playing of a problem situation. For instance, the class could be told that four students have been elected to serve on a committee to plan the senior prom. In a meeting after school, the students begin to plan the dance, the theme, refreshments, entertainment, etc. But they drift into talking about their personal plans after graduation. At this point, the teacher could ask for volunteers to participate in the dramatization. Each "actor" would receive a 3″ x 5″ card providing limited background information similar to the following:

BRAD EDWARDS: You have been working after school, Saturdays, and summers the past two years in a large bakery. You have had little time to date, and you have held down other expenditures. You have been trying to save enough money to attend the junior college in town next year. You want to finish college very much, and you are willing to work hard and to make many sacrifices to reach this goal. Your parents will not be able to give you any financial help, as your father makes a low salary and there are three other, younger children in your family. Your father and mother think you should get a full-time job and pay room and board next year at home to help out.

CHERYL KELLY: You have thought about college. You have made fairly good grades. But you have been dating a young man for a year who is a sophomore in college. You would like to get married. Yet if you are married, it would be impossible for both you and your boyfriend to complete college. You are thinking of going to work so you can get married and help the young man finish college.

THELMA MENDES: You are definitely going to college. Your parents put away money for your college through an investment plan started when you were born. There is enough money in the fund to send you to an eastern school your mother attended. While you do want to go to college, it seems to you that you have always been going to school. You would like to use part of the money to go to Europe for the entire summer and then go to a state university quite close to home. By cutting down on your college costs you can make the trip. Your parents think there is plenty of time for the trip and that you should go to what they consider to be the better school.

BOB PEPINSKY: You have decided that you want a new car more than an education. Your math teacher has told you that you have sufficient ability to secure a scholarship and to get a student loan. He says that you should go to college. But several of your close friends have bought cars since they were graduated from high school, and you want one. You have had to double date with these friends because you had no car of your own and because your father uses the family car to go to work on the swing shift.

As the role-playing session unfolds, the rest of the class should listen for and jot down illustrations of economic decision-making at the personal level. Ultimately, the session might conclude with a discussion centered upon the similarities between the types of problems experienced by individuals on a relatively narrow level and those encountered by industry and government which are, of course, more complex and considerably broader in scope

A number of other dimensions of the unlimited wants-limited resources generalization might also be investigated, subject to the age, maturity, and experiential base of learners. The Bucks County, Pennsylvania, schools, for example, have recently reproduced a booklet for their teachers which contains many entries from Sears Roebuck catalogs published in 1914.[24] Students of intermediate grades and above might study the catalog and categorize the types of items offered for sale. They could then compare a modern catalog with the 1914 edition, looking in particular for indications of both permanence and change in people's economic needs, wants, and desires. Students should rapidly discover that while many categories would be fundamentally similar (that is, clothing, tools, furniture, toys, etc), many completely new listings would appear in the modern catalog. For example, the tremendous enthusiasm many people have today for camping is reflected in page after page of items related to that activitiy—including pop-up-tents, gas stoves and lanterns, portable ice boxes, folding cups, air mattresses and insulated sleeping bags, etc. Students may also observe that some items offered for sale in contemporary catalogs to satisfy more common wants would have been considered only by the wealthy back in 1914. As a case in point, a modern Sears catalog has a section on works of art from which fairly expensive paintings—both originals and prints—may be purchased. A variety of types of swimming pools are offered for sale; boats, golf equipment, and other expensive sports and recreation gear have become major sellers; and a citizen of the 1960's may even plan a world-wide tour with the help of a Sears catalog! On the other hand, knickerbockers, washboards, "solid brass lampburners," "Stanley Double Farm Harnesses," and many other items are no longer wanted by most people today and are, therefore, no longer listed or produced.

No treatment of a generalization concerned with unlimited wants and limited resources could be considered complete without some handling of the idea of supply and demand. As a means of introducing second, third, and fourth graders to facets of this topic, the teacher might save a variety of grocery advertisements during a nine or ten week period, or simply record the prices of sample items throughout that time. A given brand of a specific item would be identified for each child. For example, Billy would have Crunch-Munch potato chips; Stevie, Home-Run hot dogs; Larry, Farmer Brown's bacon; Barbara, Happy Cow milk; Kevin, Yummy-Tummy ice cream; Kim, Igloo frozen orange juice; Harvey, Fruit Boat bananas; Laurie, Sweety-Pie sugar; Gail, Snowstorm flour; and Mary, Shoot-O spray starch. (Fictitious names have been used here, but real brand names would be selected for this activitiy.) Using a box of crayons, the teacher would reserve a single color for every youngster.

---

24 This booklet, entitled *1914*, may be obtained by writing to the Bucks County Public Schools, Doylestown, Pennsylvania.

Again, by way of illustration, Jimmy could have red for Wiley's tomato catsup, and Betty could have purple for Birthday-Time cake mix to easily and quickly find "his" product when it appears in a grocery ad. The supermarket data would be printed on cards taped along one wall of the classroom. A big date would be printed on a card attached to each page. By data, each primary grader would record the prices of his item.

Every pupil would be asked to report his findings. The teacher could then ask the children if they noticed anything about the prices of various products. Class members might respond that some of the prices went "up and down," while others seemed to "stay about the same." At this point, the teacher could ask for "some guesses" about why certain prices fluctuated and others remained relatively stable. Many explanations or hypotheses might be offered, and each possibility would be discussed. As a "homework" assignment, every youngster could be asked to talk with "whoever does the shopping at your house" to learn what reasons were offered for differences and similarities in prices. The next morning, the class could have a follow-up discussion on the explanations. Below are a few possibilities relevant to supply and demand which parents and others might identify and which the children could share and probe. Adjacent to each of these hypothetical statements we have offered simplified economic interpretations in adult terms. These interpretations should assist the teacher in her efforts to guide children into drawing a few elementary understandings out of their diverse contributions.

STATEMENT BY SHOPPERS	ECONOMIC INTERPRETATIONS
"The prices on many things I buy do not change very much. I guess this is because people like Mom usually need these things. They buy them often. These things are made all the time. They are always in the store. I suppose the people who make and sell them know how much to charge for them. I get used to prices marked on a lot of things."	*There is a steady demand for some products, and the supply has been adjusted to this demand. With a stable supply-demand condition, a constant price level is established. If, for many reasons, the demand should lessen, for a time there might be an oversupply; and the prices would go down. If, on the other hand, the demand should rise sharply, prices would go up until the supply could be increased to meet the demand. (This assumes that there is a "free market" situation, of course.) It is*

also quite likely that, in a situation such as this, a free competitive market does not exist. That is, the seller may, either singly or together with other producers of the same product, control or fix prices at a level that yields satisfactory profits to the producers.

"There are times when farmers decide to raise a lot of one thing such as tomatoes or peas or when they have a very big crop. Sometimes, too, more farmers decide to raise chickens, turkeys, sheep, pigs, and beef cattle or produce more milk and eggs. When more things come in from the farm, these things are often cheaper. Also, once in a while farmers raise or produce less of something, there is too much or too little moisture in the ground, a hail storm or a freeze destroys their crops, or they cannot get enough pickers. Then, I usually have to pay more for the things we want to eat."

The supply of certain grocery items is dependent upon farming practices and agricultural conditions. A large supply of farm products may exceed the immediate demand for them, thus creating the possibility of reduced prices, and vice versa. (This, of course, ignores farm price supports on certain items and other factors which could not be handled at this level.)

"Some crops are 'in season' only at certain times of the year. Do you remember that we eat a lot of watermelon in the summer but that we don't have it the rest of the year? At the first and last of the growing season there is less watermelon, so the people who really want it have to pay more for it. Watermelon costs a lot less in the middle of the season when there is a lot of it. If Mother buys ear corn in season, it costs less than if she buys it frozen at other

Again, when the demand exceeds the supply, prices rise. When the supply exceeds the demand, prices fall.

times of the year. If I buy field-
ripened tomatoes in season, they
cost less than when I buy tomatoes
raised in hothouses—you know,
like the the greenhouse where we
saw the pretty flowers? In a way,
it is the same with bananas. If
there are only a few nice bunches
of bananas in the supermarket,
they cost more. If the store has
lots and lots of them—bananas
come to the United States from
other countries on big boats, you
know—they cost less. The store has
to sell them in a hurry, too, as they
turn brown and spoil quickly."

"Once in a while, the man who
runs the supermarket wants to sell
something new. People do not
know about this new food, or soap,
or whatever it is. The man may
sell it at a cheap price at first so
people will buy it and try it. If the
people like it, they may buy it
again and again, even for a higher
price."

*There is no existing demand for
some new products, so that demand must be created through
advertising, free samples, pricing,
etc. The initial supply of the commodity may exceed the demand,
and prices are lower. If the demand for the new item then increases, the price may be raised
to that point where people will
still continue to buy the product
in order to satisfy their newly
created want. In some instances,
however, the demand for a new
product may be immediate and
substantial and may exceed the
supply. In this case, the price may
be high initially and may then
diminish as the supply increases.*

Another approach to the idea of supply and demand should hold an
unusual appeal for primary grade children. It would require the cooperation of a local pet shop operator. If the man could not come to class, a
visit would be made to his store. In either event, the primary graders
could examine and play with two puppies. One would be a mixed breed;

the other, a rare, expensive purebred. The children should observe that both of the dogs appear to be healthy, lively, and happy. The mixed breed could be identified as puppy "A," and the purebred as puppy "B." Each child would receive two 3″ x 5″ cards from the teacher, one with an "A" at the top, and the other with a "B." Every youngster would then be asked to estimate the price of each dog, and the teacher would help each class member record estimates on the cards. Next, the teacher would read first the "A" and then the "B" figures. At this point, the pet store owner would tell the children the correct prices. For purposes of illustration, it might be assumed that the mixed breed would sell for $15, while the registered dog would sell for $100. Then, the class could be asked to try to explain why the two puppies would have such *different* prices. The pet store operator would be asked to help the group explore possibilities, but the teacher might request that he respond to children's questions with *only* "Yes" or "No" answers. Following an inquiry style of questioning, the primary graders should discover that the purebred costs more to produce and therefore will be supplied only at a higher price. They are scarce relative to the (low) demand for them. The puppies are not *really* "the same." The price of the two dogs has been influenced by supply and demand factors.

Similarly, students at a variety of instructional levels might increase their understanding of the supply-demand relationship by being formed into committees which would visit different kinds of retail operations. One committee might talk with a real estate man; another, a jeweler; another, a furrier; another, a foreign sports car dealer; another, an antique store owner. With younger pupils, a parent might be asked to drive and escort a committee. Committees would be carefully briefed to look for differences in the costs of specific items. Questions such as these could be asked:

Why does one lot cost more than another?
Why does a diamond cost more than a zircon?
Why is mink more expensive than rabbit?
Why does a Jaguar cost more than an M-G?
Why does a spinning wheel cost more than a boot puller?

Experiences such as these are practical, real-life illustrations that should serve to clarify and reinforce some grasp of the supply-demand idea.

Students from the intermediate grades on up might look into supply and demand in still a different way. The law of supply and demand operates, of course, with reference to goods *and* services. The "Yellow Pages" of a telephone directory are obviously a fertile source of the services available in a community. Each student might be given a letter of the alphabet or a portion of the section headed by a particular letter and asked, as a homework assignment, to record the *services* listed under his category in a telephone directory. If the school is located in a metropolitan area, services such as the following might be recorded by a student under "L":

Labor Relations Consultants	Letter Shop Service
Laboratories-Analytical	Lettering
Laboratories-Medical	Libraries
Laboratories-Research	License Services
Laboratories-Testing	Lightning Protection
Ladders-Renting	Limousine Service
Lamps-Repairing	Linen Supply Service
Land Leveling	Linoleum Layers
Landscape Designers	Liquidators
Lathe Repairs	Lithographers
Laundries	Livestock Dealers
Laundries-Self-Service	Livestock Exchangers
Laundry Machinery-Repair	Livestock Order Buyers
Lawn Maintenance Service	Livestock Remedies
Lawn Mower-Sharpening & Repairing	Loans
Leasing Service	Locksmiths
Leather Cleaning	Luggage Repair
Leather Goods-Repairing	Lumber Treating

A listing such as this might then be compared with the listings in the Yellow Pages in a smaller community. Obviously, the larger community will offer a greater variety of services. The class might then discuss the reasons for abundance in a metropolitan area. The teacher might ask the class to imagine for a moment that they are lithographers about to open a new shop. Where might they go? Where would their services be in greatest demand? Where would they be able to receive a reasonable price for their services? What *might* happen if they opened a shop in a town of about 5,000? Why? Ultimately, the class should realize that supply and demand affect *services* as well as goods, and that the best place to offer one's services for a profit will be wherever the demand (and ability to pay) for that service is greatest relative to the existing supply and providing that the costs of doing business are not too high.

Similar questions might be explored in a number of other .contexts by students at the junior and senior high school level. For example, within the framework of an American history course, the following excerpt from Captain John G. W. Dillin's book, *The Kentucky Rifle*, might be discussed in terms of *reasons* the Indians were willing to give up so many "valuable" skins to the white trader for a relatively inefficient gun:

> When the White trader invaded the Red Man's domain, he exacted a mighty profit in an exchange for his wares. A gun is said to have been paid for with a stack of furs, high as the gun was long, and as beaver were the chief furs of export from the early Colonials, an idea can readily be obtained as to the price exacted from the Indian, as northern beaver skins in Colonial days sold for about six shillings each, and such guns as traders carried were, as a matter of reason, the poorest to be had, worth perhaps twenty shillings. Thus, when the Indian piled his beaver skins by the side of a 60-inch weapon, he paid for it at the rate of about twelve hundred shillings, for, from actual measurements, we find that a pile of beaver skins 60 inches high, when laid flat and carefully stretched, will contain a little above two hundred pelts. This is when opened, stretched and dried for export. If dressed, and perhaps this was exacted in the deal, the number of skins would be still greater.[25]

Similarly, students might explore the want ad sections of newspapers, looking for those occupations that are apparently in great demand, salaries offered, etc. Conversely, they might try to develop lists of the types of jobs that are *not* mentioned in the want ads—the jobs that are apparently easily filled and for which little demand exists. (It should be made clear, however, that many positions are not filled traditionally through such advertisements; the classified section comprises a limited sampling with a number of gaps.) To the best of their abilities, they might attempt to analyze the reasons for such discrepancies as well as to compare salaries in the high demand vs. low demand occupations.

Finally, senior high school students might come to grips with various aspects of the concept of supply and demand through the use of an hypothetical problem similar to the following. Each student receives a mimeographed copy, and each would be expected to write out his responses, i.e., what *he* would do and why:

> You have been a successful automobile salesman for a number of years. You have invested money year after year in order to save enough to have your own agency. You are now ready to decide on the franchise

---

[25] 4th ed., 1959; York, Pennsylvania: George Shumway, Publisher, 1946, p. 90.

you want. You have checked around, and there are four automotive franchises you can secure. You have to study each of the possibilities carefully and come to a decision. Which franchise would you choose and why?

1.   The Columbia Motor Company, Inc. has a franchise open. The Gem automobile which Columbia manufactures sells for a moderate price. The Gem has been manufactured in the United States for over thirty years. It has been an extremely popular car year after year. You can be assured that you will have an easy car to sell. Also, Columbia has told you that it can handle orders as large as you care to make. There are a number of Columbia dealers in your city, however, so you will have considerable competition.

2.   The Exclusive Motor Car Company, Limited, also is interested in securing a dealer in your city. They manufacture the Emerald sedan with prices starting at $15,000. This car is made in another country and is regarded as one of the finest automobiles in the world. The car is carefully made and requires a minimum of upkeep. It depreciates slowly, and some older Exclusive Emerald sedans are even in demand because of their classic beauty and reliable performance. Customers are on waiting lists all over the world for Exclusives. It takes from three to seven months to fill an order. Exclusive cannot assure you that you will be able to secure cars for all of the orders you might be able to secure.

3.   You have found out, too, that a franchise can be secured from European Motor Car Company for their Frugal Five. This five-cylinder car can be supplied to you in any quantity. You can have as many cars as you can sell. However, the appearance of the car and its unusual five-cylinder engine has held only limited appeal for American consumers. The Frugal sells in the low to moderate price range, but it has not captured the fancy of Americans.

4.   And a franchise is available for Novel cars from the Novel Automotive Company in the United States. The first Novel will come out in the fall. Production will be limited because Novel has a small assembly line. When the initial hand-produced version of the Novel was shown throughout the United States people were not overly enthusiastic about its design and some of its mechanical features.

Obviously, the positive and/or negative aspects of relatively high supply, high demand; low supply, low demand; high supply, low demand; and low supply, low demand would eventually be dealt with in this example.

"I'll be fourteen come December."

"Well, fourteen from twenty-one is seven. Give that some thought. If I take you on, you'll be my bound boy for seven years. That isn't the same as being a slave but it's near to it. You'll work when I tell you to work. You'll loaf mighty little and only when I give you permission. You won't get much money, just your keep and clothing. If you run away, I'll have the law on you; and if I catch you I may clap you in jail." [28]

High school students studying American history or enrolled in a senior problems course might look at economic change in the lives of individuals through a scholarly—yet very dramatic and readable—source such as David A. Shannon's *The Great Depression*. Professor Shannon's book tells the story of this tragic economic event and period in terms of the human beings who suffered, struggled, and lived through it. In the words of the editor, "Its emphasis is the effects of the depression upon its victims, and much of the material allows the reader to see the events of the 1930's through the eyes of these victims." [29] The passages quoted below should give the senior high school teacher some feeling for the empathetic, reflective discussion possibilities inherent in Shannon's material. These excerpts came initially from an extensive study made by the WPA Division of Research which was conducted in Dubuque, Iowa, in 1937-39.

Mr. Beuscher [a fictitious name, but a real interviewee], 62 years old, had been working for 29 years for the Dubuque railroad shops when they closed in 1931. He was recalled to work at the shops after he had been unemployed for 4 years. . . .

.   .   .   .

For a year after Mr. Beuscher lost his job, the family's only cash income was the four hundred seventy-odd dollars obtained from the insurance policies [cashed in one by one at surrender values] and Mrs. Beuscher's irregular earnings [made from sewing], as contrasted with the pre-depression regular income of about $130 a month, Mr. Beuscher's full-time earnings. In spite of all the Beuschers could do to reduce expenses and to raise cash, not all of the bills could be met: payments due on the principal of [their house] mortgage and the property taxes had to be disregarded, and Mr. and Mrs. Beuscher were harassed with worry over the $68 grocery bill, for they had never before asked for credit, except from week to week. Expenditures for replacements of

28 New York: Farrar, Straus & Giroux, Inc., 1962, p. 9.

29 Copyright © 1960. Reprinted by permission of Prentice-Hall, Inc., Englewood Cliffs, New Jersey. P. *ix*.

household equipment were eliminated from the budget. By the time Mr. Beuscher returned to work, the family had almost no bedding; this was the first special item purchased when the family again had a regular income from private employment.

. . . .

. . . [By the fall of 1933] application for relief was a virtual necessity. Mr. Beuscher remembers going down to the courthouse for the first time as the hardest thing he ever had to do in his life; his hand was "on the door-knob five times" before he turned it. The investigation, which the Beuschers recognized as necessary and inevitable, was so prolonged that Mrs. Beuscher "really didn't think" that the family would ever get relief. But finally, after about 2 months, a grocery order of $4.50 was granted. . . .

Soon Mr. Beuscher was assigned as a laborer to county relief work, for which he was paid, always in grocery orders, $7.20 a week; this increased amount gave the family a little more leeway. Yet they were still without much cash. Payments even of interest on the mortgage had had to cease. Because they anticipated foreclosure of the mortgage, the Beuschers applied for a Home Owners loan, which was refused, since there seemed to be little chance of Mr. Beuscher's getting back to work. . . .

. . . .

While the relief grants continued, a married daughter whose husband, as a collection agent, found his commissions going lower and lower, and a married son, who "hadn't a sign of a job," moved in with the parents. There were then 13 living in the 7 room house. . . .[30]

Samuel P. Hays' *The Response to Industrialism: 1885-1914* is a second readable, scholarly source to which the senior high school teacher of American history might turn as a means of helping students explore economic changes in relationship to individuals. The teacher could initiate an independent student research project by reading the following from the Hays' paperback:

The history of modern America is, above all, a story of the impact of industrialism on every phase of human life. It is difficult for us today fully to imagine the implications of this change, for we did not know an earlier America firsthand. But the American of 1914 could contrast, in his own experience, the old with the new. Looking backward scarcely more than forty or fifty years, he fully recognized that his country had changed rapidly and fundamentally. He had personally experienced the transition from a society relatively untouched by industrialism to one

---

[30] *Ibid.*, pp. 138–145.

almost transformed by it. Seldom, if ever, in American history had so much been altered within the lifetime of a single man.

Had he been a manufacturer, a merchant, a laborer, or a farmer, the American of 1914 would have experienced the transition from relatively stable, local business affairs to intense nationwide competition that rendered his way of making a living far less secure. . . .[31]

After a brief discussion by the class of the above passage, the teacher would invite each student to project himself into the economic life of an individual living in 1914. Every class member could be "a manufacturer, a merchant, a laborer, or a farmer" (or another person). Using histories, biographies, autobiographies, diaries, letters, magazine articles, newspaper stories and editorials, charts and graphs, and other such materials found in the classroom and provided by the classroom teacher, the school librarian, or perhaps a neighboring college or university, a student would take "a step back in time." He would try to capture something of the economic spirit of the times and the needs, wants, aspirations, and values of an individual enveloped in the Industrial Revolution. He would concentrate especially on changes in our country's economic goals and system. As a culmination to his students' independent research activities, the teacher might develop an imaginary "public forum" or "town meeting" where class members could assume various roles they had studied and discuss some "contemporary" economic problem or issue that would have been compelling in 1914.

Shifting from the individual level to another sphere, a class investigating economic change might look at the birth, development, and maturation of a particular company or its decline and demise. This approach could be geared to the background, maturity, and sophistication of the group and handled in a more cursory fashion or tackled in some depth. Younger children might have some exposure to the growth of a small business in their community, while older students could investigate transformations that have taken place in a larger, more complex concern. We will assume for the sake of this illustration that high school students are involved in this project.

If a class studies a local company, a field trip to that operation might be arranged or a resource person invited to spend a day or two in class. In either case, a well-informed, long-time employee of the company could show the group evidence of the company's change or tell students about alterations in its way of doing business. Some larger companies have

---

[31] Chicago: The University of Chicago Press, 1957, p. 1.

orientation sessions for new employees which a few students might be permitted to attend and then review in class. Other companies have even developed slides, filmstrips, or films which tell their story and which should arouse a great deal of interest and provide worthwhile, meaningful information. There are businesses, too, that have published brochures and booklets for employees, stockholders, and others that describe their progress. And, of course, there are periodicals and books which trace the histories of given companies.

We have room here to include only one example of the kind of published material a resourceful classroom teacher could uncover to help his class study change in a company. While the book from which we have chosen to quote is entitled *Longview: The Remarkable Beginnings of a Modern Western City*, it deals not only with a city's birth and development, but it is also replete with appropriate, interesting, readable, and well-documented information on the operation of the Long-Bell Lumber Company. In fact, the company preceded, planned, and developed the city. The author, John M. McClelland, Jr., is a life-long resident of Longview, the son of one of its pioneers, and the publisher of its daily newspaper, so his story has a first-hand quality which should be appealing to high school students.

Here, then, are excerpts from McClelland's book which could be used to launch a discussion of economic change in a company:

> The beginnings go back to a carefully made decision around a conference table in Kansas City, Mo., in the year 1918.
> Robert Alexander Long called that meeting. He was the slender, tireless, soft spoken president of the Long-Bell Lumber Company, the largest retailer and manufacturer of lumber in the United States. Mr. Long realized that his company had come to a point of decision. . . .
> By 1918 the timber owned by the company in the southern states was nearly all gone. . . .
> .   .   .   .
> So Mr. Long called the "men whom we considered or called the heart of our organization to meet in the directors' room of the Long-Bell Lumber Co. for the purpose of getting their views as to whether or not they felt it advisable for the company to liquidate and go out of the maufacturing business or to continue.
> After considerable discussion each man around the long table was asked to express himself. Should the company cash in and go out of the manufacturing business or should it seek some new field to begin anew? None hesitated in his answer. Each voted to go ahead.

If they had known what lay ahead in the western venture that was to result from that decision, this group of lumbermen might not have voted as they did. If they could have foreseen the hard work that was to be the lot of several of them for the next 30 years of their lives, the disappointments as well as the triumphs, the crippling economic depression that was to strike just at the time when full success seemed at hand, the immensity of the task of building not just saw-mills but an entire city, would they have gone ahead?

. . . .

Southern lumbermen learned long ago that it is far more profitable to cut good quality timber than poor. So Long-Bell set out to search for good timber once the decision had been made to head west. . . .

. . . .

. . . Then the party took off into the virgin forest of northern Cowlitz County—such timber as men used to the little trees of the south had never seen before. Here, standing in thick groves, were towering timber giants that had been growing for centuries. Some reached up 200 feet or more and in the shade far below the men on horses felt very small as they followed seldom used forest paths across the hills and up over Mt. Abernethy.

The party came out of the forest a week later down Campbell creek, emptying into the Columbia. They were convinced that here indeed was the finest timber in the world. The average tree actually scaled 7,000 board feet.

. . . .

Three possible mill sites were studied. . . .

. . . .

Among the advantages [of the Cowlitz site] were:
"Good location for a town.
"Excellent possibilities to realize on increased property values of developed property.
"Possibilities of connection with Chicago, Milwaukee and St. Paul Railroad.
"Opportunities for mercantile profits.
"Most accessible to log supply of any point on Columbia to Long-Bell holdings.
"Location at point farthest down river at which all principal rail connections can be secured.
"Good location on main channel of Columbia."
Among the disadvantages listed for this site were:
"Annual dangers from freshets.
"Town site located behind dike.

"No good roads in vicinity.
"Possible difficulties with labor supply."

. . . .

. . . Municipal planners estimated that for every industrial worker in a community there would be three and a half non-industrial workers. That would mean the Long-Bell mills alone would be the means of supporting perhaps 14,000 or more persons. It was then, apparently, in January, 1922, that Mr. Long's ideas for a city began to take shape.

. . . .

The cost of the mill site was $515,002. The big second purchase came to $1,515,626, and the final acquisition cost $580,473, bringing the total for the whole valley to $2,611,103.

Pondering this total, the lumbermen from Missouri began to comprehend that suddenly, without asking for it, they had a vast real estate development as well as a new lumbering operation on their hands.

. . . .

The company was in a hurry primarily because Longview and the mills were costing more than anyone had anticipated. The sooner the mills could start sawing lumber and the quicker real estate could be sold and some of the huge investment in land recovered, the less would be the financial burden the company would have to carry.

. . . .

In 1922 Long-Bell had a net worth of $41,080,659. That was big. But by 1926 the company had spent well over $50,000,000 for Washington timber, for building mills and for the creation of a new city. That huge investment meant inevitably a big debt.

. . . .

Mr. Long waited anxiously one day in Kansas City for a telephone call from Tennant who was assembling data on the costs of building the mill. He was alone with Nelson in the director's room when the call came from Kelso. Mr. Long took the phone. The West Fir unit, together with the power house, Tennant had to report, would cost at least $11,000,000. Mr. Long sank into a chair aghast.

. . . .

To raise this money Mr. Long and the other stockholders elected to take in new partners. A bond issue of $28,000,000 and an 8 per cent preferred stock issue, amounting to $8,000,000 were sold to the public through bond houses. By 1926 some 10,000 persons instead of just a few either owned a part of the company or had a first mortgage lien on the properties.

. . . .

But whereas in 1929 the company had been able to break even, the next year it showed a loss of $2,600,000. The lumber business was one of the first to feel the worst effects of the economic depression that swept the country. For thirty years prior to 1929 lumber production in the United States had remained fairly constant, fluctuating around 35 billion feet annually. By 1932 it was down to 10 billion feet.

. . . .

. . . [The] nation sank deeper into economic depression. The lumber business along with most others got worse. Long-Bell was making lumber and selling it at less than cost just to keep the mills in Longview going three days a week with many of the men making only 25 cents an hour.

. . . .

Longview was founded in what proved to be the inflationary period after World War I, and soon after the mills started the lumber market began going downhill. It never came back to 1922 levels until after the second war. . . .[32]

Following its study of economic change in a company, a class might move right into an investigation of change in a major industry. A number of industries could be selected for this purpose, of course, but the cattle industry is an example of one which should attract and hold the interest of students—especially its earlier period which should bring to mind the television "Westerns" to which many students are addicted. Walter Prescott Webb's vivid history, *The Great Plains*, is one of the best sources a teacher could use for the "romantic" period of this industry which has had continuing importance in our economy. Here are just a few selections from Webb's book to give senior high school teachers some feeling for its possibilities:

The price situation in 1865 was as follows: cattle in Texas could be bought for $3 and $4 per head, on the average; but even so, there were no buyers. The same cattle in the Northern markets would have brought $30 or $40 . . .

. . . .

. . . [The] purpose of the Texans in making the first drives to the north was to find a market for their cattle. Their immediate objective was a railhead from which the cattle could be shipped East. . . .

. . . .

. . . In the end the cattle kingdom occupied practically the whole Great Plains environment; it was the most natural economic and social order that the white man had yet developed in his experiment with the Great Plains.

---

[32] John M. McClelland, Jr., *Longview: The Remarkable Beginnings of a Modern Western City* (Portland, Oregon: Binfords & Mort, Publishers, 1949), pp. 1, 2–3, 5, 6, 13, 16, 24–25, 44, 128, 129, 130, 132, and 138–140.

. . . .

In 1862 the Federal Homestead Law was passed; in 1874 the first piece of barbed wire was sold in the United States. These two facts combined to break the even tenor of the cattleman's way.

Until 1873 the establishment of cattle ranches in the West proceeded without interruption. Until 1870 the herds sent to Abilene and other railheads sold on a steady or rising market. Prices were particularly good in 1870, with the result that the drive from Texas in 1871 was the greatest in history—seven hundred thousand head going to Kansas alone. Besides the Texas cattle, the other Western states were beginning to contribute to the beef supply and to reap the benefits of the high prices. But in 1871 the market conditions had changed, and the drovers found almost a complete reversal of the situation of the year before. There were few buyers, and they were reluctant rather than eager purchasers. Business conditions were slackening, the currency issue was agitating the country, and the railroads had put an end to a rate war which hitherto had benefited the cattlemen. Half the cattle brought from Texas remained unsold and had to be wintered at a loss on the prairies of Kansas. . . .[33]

Moving into still another sphere, the teacher might help his students look at evidence of economic change in their own locale. This approach, of course, could be tailored to any instructional level. It could focus on simple, concrete, obvious examples of alterations that have taken and are taking place in the community; or it could employ more complex, abstract, subtle illustrations. It could range from an informal walking tour around the area where the school building is situated to an all-day field trip where students might be bused to a group of businesses and/or industries. This procedure might deal with organizational changes in the city, such as the replacement of corner grocery stores by supermarkets. Or it could be centered on technological innovations in transportation, communication, housing, food preparation and preservation, production, etc. Or it might be focused on changes in values with economic connotations, such as fair employment and housing.

In those instances where teachers have access to a local historical museum or society, students could uncover countless examples of economic change registered in photographs, documents, advertisements, etc. Students in Duluth, Minnesota, for instance, might find an old advertisement such as this one which should trigger a class discussion embodying a group of insights into economic change:

---

[33] Boston: Ginn & Company, 1931, pp. 216, 217, 226, 230–231.

3000 LABORERS
W A N T E D
On the LAKE SUPERIOR AND MISSISSIPPI RAILROAD from Duluth
at the Western Extremity of Lake Superior, to ST. PAUL
Constant Employment will be given. Wages range from $2.00 to $4.00
per Day.
MECHANICS
Are Needed at Duluth!
Wages to Masons and Plasterers, $4.00 per day; Carpenters, $3.00 per day.
10,000 EMIGRANTS
WANTED TO SETTLE ON THE LANDS OF THE COMPANY, NOW
OFFERED ON LIBERAL CREDITS AND AT LOW PRICES.

Large bodies of Government Lands, subject to *Homestead* Settlement, or open to *Pre-Emption*. These Lands offer Facilities to Settlers not surpassed, if equalled by any lands in the West. They lie *right along the line* of the Railroad connecting Lake Superior with the Mississippi River, one of the most important Roads in the West. Forty miles of the Road are now in running order, and the whole Road (150 miles) will be completed by June, 1870. WHITE and YELLOW PINE, and VALUABLE HARD-WOOD, convenient to Market, abound.

The SOIL is admirably adapted to the raising of WINTER WHEAT and TAME GRASSES. *Stock have Good Pasture until the Depth of Winter.*

The waters of Lake Superior, in connection with the Timber, make this much the warmest part of Minnesota. The navigation season at Duluth is several weeks longer than on the Mississippi. The LUMBER interest will furnish abundant and profitable WINTER WORK.

FREE TRANSPORTATION over the completed portion of the Railroad will be given to Laborers and all Settling on the Lands of the Company.

At Duluth *Emigrants* and their families will find *free* quarters in a new and commodious *Emigrant House*, until they locate themselves, by applying at Duluth to LUKE MARVIN, Agent. *Laborers* will report to WM. BRANCH, Contractor of the Road. For information as to Steamers to Duluth, inquire at Transportation Office in any of the Lake Cities.
DULUTH, MINN., JUNE 14, 1869.

Finally, economic changes at the national level could be studied in a myriad of ways by children and youth of various ages. Secondary students, for example, might begin a study of changing economic values, systems, and conditions in our nation by specializing in the administrations of our presidents. Students might be assigned a specific president and explore the economic situation of the country during his tenure. Beginning with the inaugural address, a class member could consult many sources and compose a complete economic portrait of that president's period. The following are selected passages from the inaugural addresses of various presidents which should stimulate students into further investigation. Certainly, there is evidence of economic change in these statements.

The present situation of the world is indeed without a parallel, and that of our own country full of difficulties. The pressure of these, too, is the more severely felt because they have fallen upon us at a moment when the national prosperity being at a height not before attained, the contrast resulting from the change has been rendered the more striking. . . .[34]

The great amount of our revenue and the flourishing state of the Treasury are a full proof of the competency of the national resources for any emergency, as they are of the willingness of our fellow-citizens to bear the burdens which the public necessities require. The vast amount of vacant lands, the value of which daily augments, forms an additional resource of great extent and duration. These resources, besides accomplishing every other necessary purpose, put it completely in the power of the United States to discharge the national debt at an early period. . . .[35]

. . . Under a wise policy the debts contracted in our Revolution and during the War of 1812 have been happily extinguished. By a judicious application of the revenues not required for other necessary purposes, it is not doubted that the debt which has grown out of the circumstances of the last few years may be speedily paid off.[36]

Our present financial condition is without a parallel in history. No nation has ever before been embarrassed from too large a surplus in its treasury. This almost necessarily gives birth to extravagant legislation. It

---

[34] James Madison, "First Inaugural Address," March 4, 1809, in *Inaugural Addresses of the Presidents of the United States: From George Washington 1789 to Harry S. [sic] Truman 1949* (Washington, D. C.: United States Government Printing Office, 82d Congress, 2d Session, House Document No. 540, 1952), p. 21.

[35] James Monroe, "First Inaugural Address," March 4, 1817, in *Inaugural Addresses . . .* , p. 32.

[36] James K. Polk, "Inaugural Address," March 4, 1845, in *Inaugural Addresses . . .* , p. 85.

produces wild schemes of expenditure and begets a race of speculators and jobbers, whose ingenuity is exerted in contriving and promoting expedients to obtain public money. . . .

The natural mode of relief from this embarrassment is to appropriate the surplus in the Treasury to great national objects for which a clear warrant can be found in the Constitution. . . .[37]

While a Treasury surplus is not the greatest evil, it is a serious evil. Our revenue should be ample to meet the ordinary annual demands upon our Treasury, with a sufficient margin for those extraordinary but scarcely less imperative demands which arise now and then. . . .[38]

My fellow-Citizens:

When we assembled here on the 4th of March, 1897, there was great anxiety with regard to our currency and credit. None exist now. Then our Treasury receipts were inadequate to meet the current obligations of the Government. Now they are sufficient for all public needs, and we have a surplus instead of a deficit. Then I felt constrained to convene the Congress in extraordinary session to devise revenues to pay the ordinary expenses of the Government. Now I have the satisfaction to announce that the Congress just closed has reduced taxation in the sum of $41,000,000. Then there was deep solicitude because of the long depression in our manufacturing, mining, agricultural, and mercantile industries and the consequent distress of our laboring population. Now every avenue of production is crowded with activity, labor is well employed, and American products find good markets at home and abroad.[39]

We contemplate the immediate task of putting our public household in order. We need a rigid and yet sane economy, combined with fiscal justice, and it must be attended by individual prudence and thrift, which are so essential to this trying hour and reassuring for the future.

The business world reflects the disturbance of war's reaction. Herein flows the lifeblood of material existence. The economic mechanism is intricate and its parts interdependent, and has suffered the shocks and jars incident to abnormal demands, credit inflations, and price upheavals. The normal balances have been impaired, the channels of distribution

---

[37] James Buchanan, "Inaugural Address," March 4, 1857, in *Inaugural Addresses* . . . , pp. 105–106.
[38] Benjamin Harrison, "Inaugural Address," March 4, 1889, in *Inaugural Addresses* . . . , p. 149.
[39] William McKinley, "Second Inaugural Address," March 4, 1901, in *Inaugural Addresses* . . . , p. 167.

have been clogged, the relations of labor and management have been strained. We must seek the readjustment with care and courage. . . .[40]

I am certain that my fellow Americans expect that on my induction into the Presidency I will address them with a candor and a decision which the present situation of our Nation impels. This is pre-eminently the time to speak the truth, the whole truth, frankly and boldly. Nor need we shrink from honestly facing conditions in our country to-day. This great Nation will endure as it has endured, will revive and will prosper. So, first of all, let me assert my firm belief that the only thing we have to fear is fear itself—nameless, unreasoning, unjustified terror which paralyzes needed efforts to convert retreat into advance. In every dark hour of our national life a leadership of frankness and vigor. has met with that understanding and support of the people themselves which is essential to victory. I am convinced that you will again give that support to leadership in these critical days.

In such a spirit on my part and on yours we face our common difficulties. They concern, thank God, only material things. Values have shrunken to fantastic levels; taxes have risen; our ability to pay has fallen; government of all kinds is faced by serious curtailment of income; the means of exchange are frozen in the currents of trade; the withered leaves of industrial enterprise lie on every side; farmers find no markets for their produce; the savings of many years in thousands of families are gone.

More important, a host of unemployed citizens face the grim problem of existence, and an equally great number toil with little return. Only a foolish optimist can deny the dark realities of the moment.[41]

---

4. *Every Economic System Possesses Regularities Which Make Certain Forms of Prediction Possible.*

> . . . Generalizations are dangerous. Prophecy is more dangerous. But the human mind longs for something more positive than a glimpse at a swirling tide. . . .
>
> CHARLES A. BEARD

---

[40] Warren G. Harding, "Inaugural Address," March 4, 1921, in *Inaugural Addresses* . . . , p. 201.
[41] Franklin D. Roosevelt, "Inaugural Address," March 4, 1933, in *Inaugural Addresses* . . . , p. 225.

Predicting the voting behavior of various groups is a primary concern of the political scientist. Similarly, the sociologist is involved in prognosis when he creates a device that yields data indicating that a given child may become delinquent. The geographer who helps choose the location for a new industrial plant is also predicting, as are other social scientists in an almost endless variety of situations. The economist, too, finds that prediction is essential if he is to put his theories concerning man's economic behavior to the test.

Indeed, it might be said that the fundamental task of economics (or any other discipline that labels itself a "science") is prediction—prediction that helps us decide upon *how* we can repair, maintain or improve our standard of living. This, of course, is easier said than done. Human behavior is far less predictable than is the reaction that occurs upon mixing a given chemical with another; nevertheless, predict we must if social science is to make a serious contribution to an understanding of the world in which we live.

Fortunately, the economist studying economic behavior is *not* dealing with completely random, unstructured patterns. People *do* follow certain routines; there *is* a degree of orderliness and regularity within a given society, and economic prediction *is* possible, even though (as Kenneth Boulding put it) "reality is always more complex than the economist's picture of it." [42]

Children in the middle grades of the elementary school might be introduced to the ideas of prediction and regularity through the use of some well-known proverbs. For example, the following samples of Ben Franklin's advice might be written on the chalkboard:

A penny saved is a penny earned.
A man may, if he knows not how to save,
keep his nose to the grindstone.
He that goes a borrowing goes a sorrowing.

A brief discussion of the "essential message" contained in these and other similar proverbs might take place, with the class undoubtedly concluding that saving one's money is the only avenue to fame and fortune. At this point the teacher might say something such as: "We all seem to agree that the proverbs are telling us to save our money. Let's stop and think about that for a minute. Suppose *everyone*—your mothers,

---

[42] *Economic Analysis* (New York: Harper & Row, Publishers, 1941), p. 15.

fathers, uncles. and aunts, children, policemen, firemen, storekeepers, doctors, lawyers—everyone decided to follow this advice and save all of their money except what was needed for enough food and clothing and the rent on a house or apartment. What do you think would happen?" Regardless of the trend the discussion takes, the teacher might list the local equivalents of the following businesses on the board and focus discussion on the effects of this massive savings program on each:

The Maple Leaf Drive-In Theatre
The Jones Book Store
The Four Corners Gasoline Service Station
The Central Television Sales and Service Co.
The Great Central Railroad
Nelson's Summer Resort and Lodge
Marie's Beauty Shop, etc.

Assuming that some children in the class will quickly recognize the negative effects on one or two of the listed businesses, the teacher might raise the question, "why?" That is, what is there about our system upon which people in business depend? If you were to open a gas station or a summer resort, what would *you* depend upon so far as people's spending habits are concerned? Eventually the class should conclude that while we expect people to save *some* money, many people's livelihood depends on our continued willingness to spend much of what we earn for things beyond the basic necessities.

A number of other simple situations might be explored at this grade level in terms of certain regularities or patterns of economic behavior and, therefore, the possibilities of prediction. For example, let us assume there is a severe cold snap in Florida during the height of the grapefruit growing season. Can we predict what may happen to grapefruit prices? Why is this possible? Or, the Congress has just passed a bill reducing taxes on automobiles and luggage. What is likely to happen to the sale of such items? Why? Imagine a "typical" American family, mother, father, and three children, living in a suburban community with an income of about $7500 per year. Can we guess many of the things for which the family is likely to spend its money? How are we able to make such guesses? Here, too, the children should begin to see that, for our society, we can make reasonably intelligent guesses about the economic behavior of people in general.

The twin ideas of regularity and prediction might also be approached through a number of simple children's books.

J. M. Goodspeed's *Let's Take a Trip to Watch a Building Go Up* [43] offers primary grade children an opportunity to make such predictions at their level of understanding. It begins with a simple introduction to the need for new construction, and then takes the reader through a series of steps showing different types of jobs or occupations involved in a building's planning and construction. The story might be approached by having children think about the meaning or the implications of the construction of a new building. Can we guess what it might mean to other people? Who will be likely to get jobs and earn money? What kinds of things would workers do? How is the construction of a new building good for some people? Could it be bad for some people, too? In what ways? Again, the focus here is that we can predict, with a good deal of certainty, that a new building project will mean jobs for many people, incomes for their families, and more money spent for other things by those earning wages through such construction.

Adele Nathan's *The Building of the First Transcontinental Railroad* should provide older children with a similar opportunity to hypothesize about the implications of building a railroad. In particular, the class might be asked to think about the predictions the railroad's backers must have made concerning the probable results of such a venture. How would they get their money back and earn a profit? What did they anticipate would happen when the road was completed? Following some discussion of these questions, this passage from the book itself might be read to the class:

. . . Today Diesel engines click over the rails where once General Jack's men fought the Indians. A great gas turbine-electric speeds over the Union Pacific lines. Its voice, a high-pitched wail like the scream of a jet, echoes through canyons where men once chipped away rock with hand-pick and shovel.

All over the country, automobiles are run with Oklahoma oil, houses are heated with Pennsylvania coal, and furnaces made from Minnesota iron. Almost everything you use or eat comes from some distant place and, nine chances out of ten, it came as freight on a railroad train.

Anybody can sit down today in San Francisco, Chicago or New York, and eat grapefruit from Texas, strawberries from California, oranges

---

[43] New York: G. P. Putnam's Sons, 1956.

from Florida, tomatoes from Maryland, and beef from Kansas. The meal can be topped off with Vermont cheese and Washington apples. This isn't a special party like the feast at the Hundredth Meridian. It's just an ordinary meal, delivered to you every day by the American railroads.

If you're ever lucky enough to make the trip across the continent by rail, it will seem to you that the corn and the wheat fields of Kansas, Nebraska and the Dakotas never stop. All through Colorado and Montana, cattle along the right of way stop chewing long enough to turn their white faces and look after the Iron Horse. They aren't frightened as the Indian ponies were. The cattle are used to seeing trains.

You go through big towns like Butte and Denver and Lincoln and Minneapolis that might not be there at all if it weren't for the railroad. Even Omaha would probably still be a "handful of matchboxes" out in the middle of what used to be nowhere before the trains came.[44]

Clara Judson's *St. Lawrence Seaway* is another example of the kind of book intermediate grade children might use to explore predictive uses of economic data. The "logic" of the seaway proposal is summed up in the following passage:

1. A demand does exist for a deep waterway. At least seventeen states will be directly affected; their population is about one third of the United States. Farmers, industrialists, and all recent presidents favor the work.
2. The national economy requires more transport. Railroad rates are high; railroad transport is inadequate, especially at crop-moving time.
3. Water transport is cheap and excellent for bulk products—ore, grain, coal, oil. The question is not between two sorts of transport, both rail and water are needed. The St. Lawrence Waterway is already in use; it needs only improving. The expense, while considerable, is small compared with benefits.
4. An improved waterway would bring ocean-going ships into the Middle West. The whole nation will benefit.[45]

The planners of the seaway were apparently right on all counts, and our ability to make predictions of this kind looms increasingly important as other complex ventures are contemplated.

---

[44] From *The Building of the First Transcontinental Railroad*, by Adele Nathan (A Landmark Book). Copyright 1950 by Adele Nathan. Reprinted by permission of Random House, Inc.
[45] Chicago: Follett Publishing Company, 1959, p. 98. Permission granted by Follett Publishing Company.

The ways in which businessmen use the regularities of our system to predict their costs and their profits might easily be explored in the intermediate grades through a "case study" approach. The class could be told that four children—Janis, Betsy, Billy and Danny—have decided to open a soft drink stand near Janis' house. Their stand will be on a shady street which is near a large neighborhood shopping center. Many cars go by, and it ought to be a good place to sell cool drinks. Betsy has some big, heavy paper boxes to make a stand. Billy can borrow three glass pitchers from his mother, and Danny will furnish the ice-cubes. After talking things over, the children decide to purchase the following:

Frozen grape juice	2 cans for 25¢
Frozen orange juice	2 cans for 39¢
Frozen lemonade	2 cans for 20¢
4 oz. paper cups	50 cups for 29¢
Felt tip pen to write signs	59¢
Posterboard for signs	25¢

At this point the teacher might suggest that each member of the class attempt to figure out expenses and arrive at a price for each cup of fruit drink that would allow the four partners to make a profit. Some children might suggest a figure such as 6 or 7 cents a cup, settling for what appears to be a rather small profit and keeping the price low enough to entice customers. Others may suggest a higher price so that they will be "sure" to make money. *Everyone* ought to try to figure out how much profit he would make at his chosen price, however. After the children have estimated their profits the teacher supplies this added information:

1. At the end of the day Billy accidentally knocked down and broke one of the pitchers. It cost 75¢.
2. Not all the lemonade was sold. The four partners each drank three cups apiece.

Each child then looks at his figures to see whether a profit has, indeed, been made. In most cases, money will have been lost. Now the teacher raises the fundamental question which is, of course, what was wrong with our predictions? What do big businesses have to consider when *they* set a price for their products? (waste, equipment replacement and repair, insurance, cost of light, heat, rental, advertising, and salaries.) Do most businesses seem to predict accurately? How do you know?

Older students might explore aspects of this fifth generalization by investigating a real or hypothetical situation involving the addition or perhaps discontinuance of a transportation facility in a community. In recent years, many communities have experienced controversy that arises over the construction of a new thruway that by-passes a small town; the halting of railroad service to a community that has had such service for over 50 years; the addition of air transportation to the travel facilities of a middle-sized community. Students with library access to newspapers such as the *New York Times* might study the arguments offered by both sides when the New York, New Haven and Hartford Railroad decided to drop service in a number of New England communities. Prior to the data-gathering stage of such an investigation, however, the students ought to try to predict as many implications of such a development as possible. Given certain understandings about how the American economy works, what might we guess would happen to such communities? What does a railroad mean to a town? What problems might this create for some individuals? For various businesses? Eventually, their guesses might be compared to the predictions made by involved citizens, representatives of the railroad, and others, which were printed in the *Times*. A *continued* study of succeeding issues of the newspaper as well as other sources might corroborate some predictions and negate others.

Another related approach that would be suitable for senior high school students might involve the problems of prediction that are involved whenever government (national, state or local) makes decisions dealing with the community's economic affairs. Quite obviously, the testimony that was written into the Congressional Record prior to the passage of the federal government's massive tax cut in 1964 as well as the more recent excise tax cut of 1965 offers the more mature student a fertile field for studying and gathering information illustrating the significance of economic prediction in running our country's affairs.

Continuing on the national level, the much debated Tennessee Valley Authority offers still another case history for investigation by mature students. At its inception, a number of predictions were made, based upon data available to government economists and others, concerning the benefits such a project would bring to the valley and the nation as a whole. Joseph S. Ransmeier, in his *The Tennessee Valley Authority: A Case Study in the Economics of Multiple Purpose Stream Planning* discusses the positive results of the predictions of TVA economists concerning new approaches to the retailing of electrical power:

. . . Certainly the outstanding lesson to the economist of the TVA resale rate program and the experience of the privately owned companies in retailing "cheap" electricity has been the responsiveness of consumption to rate reductions. Indeed, in the domestic and commercial fields the sensitivity of power demand to downward price adjustments seems to have been so great that it is surprising that the privately owned companies had not experimented more in the possibilities of promotional rate making.[46]

Ransmeier's book offers the advanced student a wealth of data dealing with planning and carrying out a real project, solidly based upon modern economic theory, in which reasonably accurate predictions were made about a number of economic factors.

Similarly, local or statewide projects and programs often offer fruitful opportunities to study the feasibility of economic prediction in our society, as well as the kinds of data and research techniques used by economists. The recent passage of Minnesota's controversial "Taconite Amendment" could serve as a particularly interesting case study for Midwestern high school students. Proponents of the measure predicted that a guaranteed tax exemption for a period of years would bring about the construction of taconite plants in the poverty stricken iron-range areas of northern Minnesota. In this case, too, newspapers published during the 1963 session of the state legislature (particularly the *Minneapolis Star and Journal*) offer the most readily available sources of information concerning arguments for and against the amendment. Again, however, we have a situation in which predictions were made on the basis of observed regularities in our economic system, and, at this writing, the sponsors of the amendment seem to have predicted with a high degree of accuracy.

Another approach that offers possibilities for exploring ways in which economists use regularities in economic prediction involves the study of government agencies. Perhaps groups of students in a high school class might each select an agency for study from among the following:

1. The Federal Reserve Board
2. The Interstate Commerce Commission
3. The Federal Power Commission
4. The Department of Agriculture
5. The Bureau of Mines
6. The Federal Housing Administration

[46] Nashville: Vanderbilt University Press, 1942, p. 167.

The group selecting the Federal Reserve Board could, during its investigation, focus on the role credit plays in our society. Would it, for example, be possible for the Board to operate successfully *without* the knowledge that the American public and business community can be expected to behave in certain ways so far as credit purchasing is concerned? Can members of the Board assume that the wants, needs, and buying habits of Americans will not suddenly change—that they follow certain patterns which make the Board's adjustments reasonable and logical? Similarly, the other agencies can regulate only because they make certain assumptions about the nature of our system as a whole, and an investigation of some of these assumptions could comprise an exceedingly valuable activity for older students. Students might investigate as well the assumptions upon which such Federal programs as the Area Re-development Act of 1961 or the Manpower Development and Training Act of 1962 were based, looking critically at the degree of success or failure demonstrated so far.

In a negative sense (and with the perspective of history), high school students might examine carefully and reflectively the assumptions about the American economic system that made the following suggestions possible. They are, in effect, predictions concerning the best means of dealing with the depression of the 1930's and were part of *both* the Republican and Democratic parties' platforms in the 1932 election:

REPUBLICAN

. . . Constructive plans for financial stabilization cannot be completely organized until our national, State and municipal governments not only balance their budgets but curtail their current expenses as well to a level which can be steadily and economically maintained for years to come.

We urge prompt and drastic reduction of public expenditures and resistance to every appropriation not demonstrably necessary to the performance of government, national or local . . .

DEMOCRAT

. . . We advocate an immediate and drastic reduction of governmental expenditures by abolishing useless commissions and offices, consolidating departments and bureaus, and eliminating extravagance, to accomplish a saving of not less than twenty-five per cent in the cost of federal government, and we call upon the Democratic Party in the States to make a zealous effort to achieve a proportionate result.

We favor maintenance of the national credit by a federal budget annually balanced on the basis of accurate executive estimates within revenues, raised by a system of taxation levied on the principle of ability to pay . . .[47]

Most junior and senior high school students are undoubtedly aware that *individuals* (as well as corporations or governments) often try to analyze economic conditions and predict future trends. For some, such predictions are soundly based and result in "fame and fortune"; for others, the outcome has been financial loss or ruin.

Henry Ford is perhaps a classic example of a man who analyzed existing economic conditions both shrewdly and successfully. Junior high school students might be asked to examine the following account of Ford's production of the historic Model T car, seeking in particular, evidence of Ford's understanding of people and their economic behavior as well as examples of his "unorthodox" (but highly successful) economic concepts:

. . . What he wanted was the simplest possible mechanism. It must have the fewest parts, be the easiest to understand and repairable with string and hairpins. It must be rugged, powerful, built to carry a family long distances up and down hills, over the roughest roads. There must be nothing fancy about it. The uglier the better . . . Ford's car must look what it was, utilitarian, the sort of thing millionaires would run away from. It must be painted black.

Once you get that frozen pattern you could spend all your time, money and effort, not improving the car, but improving the methods of turning it out. The idea of making a new model every year was uneconomical. It would mean a new annual cost of retooling your factory. If you went on producing the same thing year after year you could constantly cheapen its cost and so reduce its price.

The car Ford finally decided upon he called the Model T. When, in accordance with his plan, Ford lowered the price, the stockholders were worried.

"You mean to reduce the price every year?" they asked, in effect.

"That is my intention."

"How then will you make money?"

"By selling more cars."

"But your improved machinery will cost money. It will have to be financed. How will you do that?"

"By using the money I get for the cars to increase my plant."

"Then what happens to the profits?"

"They are to be plowed back into the works."

[47] Edward H. Merrill, *Responses to Economic Collapse* (Boston: D. C. Heath & Company, 1964), pp. 68–69, 76.

This was not orthodox business. Profits went to stockholders, not into machinery. But Ford had no faith in orthodox finance. He was suspicious of Wall Street. It was full of rich men—not good, common Americans. Their idea was to finance first and produce afterwards. Ford's way was to produce first and then finance your further production with what you made from your original sales . . .

. . . .

The Model T went into production in 1909. In 1913, production was a thousand cars a day. In 1915 the one-millionth Ford car came off a moving assembly line.

. . . .

. . . On every detail of the car Ford had guessed right. Simple, ugly, black, rugged; it was what people wanted. The company was swamped with orders. Enormous expansion would be necessary if half the demand was to be met. Henry Ford knew that it could be done by skilled mechanics. He knew, however, that there was such a thing in the world as mass production. So he got men who understood the system as it had been used to make other machines and had them install it for the biggest mass-production operation in history. To one engineer, he offered a twenty-thousand-dollar bonus over and above his salary if he could produce ten thousand cars the first year. The challenge was met. By the time the ten thousandth car came from the Ford factory the unique system had begun which, some five years later, became celebrated throughout the world.[48]

Senior high school students might enjoy participating in a practical and reasonably realistic activity designed to immerse them in both the prediction process and the machinations of the American stock market. To start, the teacher might write to any leading stockbroker in his community, seeking descriptions of a number of businesses which are trying to attract investors. This material contains predictions concerning corporations' estimated growth and anticipated future investments, as well as specific data dealing with the demand both at home and abroad for the firm's products. Each student should read *all* of the material carefully. After such study (and, we presume, the investigation and clarification of some unfamiliar, technical words) a student might imagine that he has $1000 for possible investment. The student may put all of his money into one company or invest in a number of businesses. A date is set for the completion of the project (perhaps six months from its inception) and careful records are kept, based on data obtained from the financial pages

[48] Abridged from *Machines That Built America,* by Roger Burlingame, pp. 191-194. Copyright, 1953, by Roger Burlingame. Reprinted by permission of Harcourt, Brace & World, Inc.

of the *New York Times, Wall Street Journal*, or any other newspaper containing an adequate financial page. Students may "sell" at any time, if they choose. Eventually, each student might give a report in class summarizing his current financial status. In particular, the student should focus on the *predictive* nature of his project, i.e., on the bases he used to decide on certain purchases, on the ways in which he was right, on the sources of his errors, and on factors which may have entered into the situation that he failed to consider. The following are samples of the kinds of information contained in two easily obtainable publications:

GENERAL MOTORS CORPORATION

The long-range outlook for General Motors is believed to be favorable. Supported by the increasing population and the high rate of scrappage of old vehicles, underlying demand for automobiles is expected to continue growing in coming years with possible intermediate fluctuations. As the largest maker of motor vehicles in the world, General Motors appears to be in excellent position to benefit from the growth of the industry. We believe the company's strong participation in important foreign markets enhances its long-term prospects.

FIRST NATIONAL CITY BANK

Total assets, loans, and deposits all reached new highs in 1964. Deposits, aided by the increased rate that First National City began paying on savings on January 1, 1965, are expected to continue expanding this year. If conditions remain favorable for the general economy, we believe demand for loans will increase further. These conditions and the benefits of a further reduction in the corporate tax rate indicate another gain in earnings this year. We believe, however, that the increased costs stemming from higher rates paid on deposits may modify the rate of earnings improvement during 1965 in relation to the growth of nearly 13% that Citibank achieved last year. The Administration's recent request that banks in the United States limit their foreign loans is expected to cause some shifts in the loan portfolio; at this early date, however, indications are that the impact on earnings would not be substantial.

While students may be well aware of the positive possibilities offered by a thorough knowledge of economic patterns, they should recognize, however, that even the most cautious predictions *can* go astray. Predictions involving human beings are always somewhat uncertain, and as a sobering companion to the exercise described above, the teacher might distribute the following excerpt from the October 30, 1929, issue of the *New York Times*:

Stock prices virtually collapsed yesterday, swept downward with gigantic losses in the most disastrous trading day in the stock market's history. Billions of dollars in open market values were wiped out as prices crumbled. . . .

Efforts to estimate yesterday's market losses in dollars are futile . . . However, it was estimated that 808 stocks, on the New York Stock Exchange, lost between $8,000,000,000 and $9,000,000,000 yesterday. . . .

Groups of men, with here and there a woman, stood . . . watching spools of ticker tape unwind and as the tenuous paper with its cryptic numerals grew longer at their feet their fortunes shrunk. Others sat stolidly on tilted chairs in the customers' rooms of brokerage houses and watched a motion picture of waning wealth as the day's quotations moved silently across a screen.

It was among such groups as these, feeling the pulse of a feverish financial world whose heart is the Stock Exchange, that drama and perhaps tragedy were to be found. . . . The crowds about the ticker tape, like friends around the bedside of a stricken friend, reflected in their faces the story the tape was telling. There were no smiles. There were no tears either. Just the camaraderie of fellow-sufferers. Everybody wanted to tell his neighbor how much he had lost. Nobody wanted to listen. It was too repetitious a tale. . . .

Finally, and as a climax to a class's investigation of economic prediction within the *American* system, the students might attempt to peer into our country's economic future. This experience could be undertaken (at differing levels of sophistication) by children in grades six through twelve. It involves making a broad series of predictions closely related to future economic activity in the United States. Each student might attempt to list a series of factors that will probably alter the economic situation in the future. For example, students might cite the following:

increase in desire for two cars per family
increase in birth rate
increase in world-wide travel
increase in desire for imported goods of all kinds
increase in general salary levels
increase in automation
increase in demand for power
decrease in natural resources
increase in number of people over 65
increase in leisure time

On the basis of these patterns, students might try to write a sweeping report on what life will be like in the year 2000. Possibly they might anticipate the creation of a whole series of new synthetics, a tremendous increase in the use of atomic power and new roles for government in problems related to medical aid, old age, unemployment, and poverty.

All of the preceding suggestions involve, of course, predictions based upon anticipated regularities within our own economic system. Both elementary and secondary school students ought to be aware, however, that once we move *outside* of our system, we can no longer count on similar patterns of behavior. Students at a variety of age levels can begin to grasp this idea through a number of simple experiences that are closely related to aspects of their formal curriculum. For example, in studying the Indians of the American Northwest, the teacher might emphasize the nature of the potlatch. The destruction of wealth by an individual in order to assert his superiority over another is a normal, regular predictable pattern of economic behavior among such Indians. A group of Northwest Indians might find it difficult, indeed, to understand and predict the behavior of a typical American in such circumstances, and most Americans would find it equally difficult to "get along" financially in such a society without changing their economic habits. The tendency to bargain about prices that exists in a number of cultures often results in an American tourist's paying higher prices. On the other hand, imagine what would happen if a visitor from India attempted to "bargain" with a clerk in an American department store over the price of an item!

Children might attempt to gauge their own and their classmates' reactions if they were to suddenly see a sign advertising "Sale on Ant Larvae, Insect Grubs, and Locusts." Similarly, Mongolians are generally revolted by coffee and would largely ignore a "sale" that cut coffee prices in half. Many Frenchmen would not purchase cranberry sauce at *any* price. Discussions of situations such as these may help children realize that one cannot predict economic patterns in one society on the basis of "behavioral regularities" that exist within another.

5. In a Modern, Complex Economic System, Individuals Are Dependent Upon Others for the Satisfaction of Many of Their Needs and Wants.

. . . Man lives by co-operating with his fellow men. In the modern world, that co-operation is of a boundless range and an indescribable complexity. Yet it is essentially undesigned and uncontrolled by man.

The humblest inhabitant of Great Britain or the United States depends for the satisfaction of his simplest needs upon the activities of innumerable people, in every walk of life and in every corner of the globe. The ordinary commodities which appear upon his dinner table represent the final product of the labours of a medley of merchants, farmers, seamen, engineers, workers of almost every craft. . . .[49]

The words above—written by Sir Hubert Henderson, Drummond Professor of Political Economy at Oxford University until his death in 1952—were first published in 1922. They were true and insightful then, but they are even more so today. An individual living in the 'sixties still has his own unique needs and wants and his private version of what constitutes the "most liveable life" and how it might be approached; but—like it or not—he is more and more a smaller and smaller part of a bigger and bigger economic system involving countless others. His actions may affect an ever-increasing number of fellow human beings, just as what they do can touch his life. Interdependence, then, is a basic characteristic of a contemporary, multifaceted economic system.

Teachers at all instructional levels can expose students to the idea of economic interdependence through the use of appropriate literature. A primary teacher, for example, could use *Two Is a Team* by Lorraine and Jerrold Beim to launch a discussion on mutual dependence, emphasizing in particular this passage:

"Why don't we get a job?" Ted said. They went into the grocery store. "Could you use two delivery boys?" they asked.

"Well, I could," the man behind the counter said, "but you have to have your own wagon to deliver the groceries."

"We haven't a wagon," Paul said. Then Ted had a wonderful idea. "We'll be back to work with a wagon tomorrow," he said.

"A wagon! Where will we get a wagon?" Paul asked when they went out. "We'll make one," Ted answered. "Out of our coasters!"

And they did! They worked hard the rest of the day building a wagon. Paul let Ted help him put the box on. Ted let Paul help him put the wheels on. And together they made a fine strong wagon! [50]

The fifth grade teacher teaching a unit on pioneers and the westward movement could use Irene Estep's *Pioneer Sodbuster* to develop a

---

[49] Sir Hubert Henderson, *Supply and Demand* (Chicago: The University of Chicago Press, 1958), pp. 2-3. World publishing rights granted by James Nisbet & Company Limited and The Cambridge University Press.

[50] New York: Harcourt, Brace & World, Inc., 1945. Pages not numbered.

number of understandings, including the idea of interdependence. Following the reading and discussion of the passage below, the children might be asked to find other examples in their reading and to share them in class.

> "This looks bad for us," Mr. Thomas said. "Do you think we should try to get through?"
> "As long as we work together we have a good chance," Mr. Warden said.
> "Why is Father unhitching Ned and Bill?" Matilda asked. "Is he going to leave us here?"
> "No," said Mark. "You watch Father now. You will see what he is going to do."
> "Your father is hitching Ned and Bill in front of Mr. Thomas' team," Mrs. Warden said. "The double team will pull the Thomas' wagon through that deep mudhole ahead."
> Mr. Warden climbed onto the Thomas wagon. All the horses stepped forward, and the Thomas wagon began to move. The wheels sank deeper and deeper into the mudhole.
>
> . . . .
>
> Just when it seemed the wheels could turn no more, the horses came to firm ground and hauled the dripping wagon out of the deep mudhole. Then the men and horses came back to get the Warden wagon.[51]

Sixth or seventh graders studying geography should enjoy and get a great deal out of Claire Huchet Bishop's sensitive and cosmopolitan book *All Alone*. A number of facets of economic dependence and interdependence could be probed and analyzed through the use of this one source, as the following selection should indicate:

> "And here we are today all gathered together. All of us are going to take a step, which, I dare say, is going to change even the look of this valley. The land of our valley is good, but it has been going to waste for a long time. Why does it not feed us any more? The trouble is that each man's fields are too small and too scattered. That's what we ourselves figured out as we talked it over all together, time and time again, when we met at one another's homes during the past winter evenings. And finally we came to a momentous decision. Of our own free will—" (Applause.) "Yes, of our own free will, without anyone telling us to do so, we, the people of Monestier, have decided to tear down the age-old fences and hedges which enclose and separate our fields, and to work

---

[51] Chicago: Benefic Press, 1958, pp. 45–46.

the whole land of the valley together—one common field under the sun."
(Applause.)

"That's what we have decided. How it can be done best we will
have to figure out among ourselves. We know it's not going to be easy.
It's quite an adventure. There will be plenty of discussing, arguing,
planning, organizing. It will mean a lot of hard teamwork all around for
every one of us. But it will also be great fun. We know we are on the
right track, because we are in this voluntarily, all together, touching
elbows and feeling the beats of one another's hearts." (Applause.)

"That's *what* happened, citizens. But now we come to the second
and most important question. *Who* made it happen?

. . . .

"A little child did it. If it had not been for this one"—and, to
Marcels utter confusion, the mayor pulled him up and pushed him in
front of the people—"if it had not been for Marcel Mabout, we would
all still be crouched in our own dens, peering at each other from behind
curtains." (Laughs and applause.)

"A little child showed the way, the new way of life. How did he do
it? It was all very simple. Cows from a neighbor went astray on his
pasture. What did he do? According to Monestier's old custom, he should
have shooed them off at once, washing his hands of what might happen
to them later. They had no right to be on his pasture, and if anything
happened to them while they were there he would be blamed. Of course,
if he had chased them off it was ten to one that they would wander and
break their necks. But it was none of his concern; it was the neighbor's,
whose fault it was for not watching them properly. . . .

"Marcel knew all that, and yet he did not shoo the cows off. He took
care of them right on the spot, and we can all easily imagine what it
meant and how difficult it was. Why did he do that? He thought of his
neighbor, later finding his heifers dead at the bottom of an abyss. And
though, in keeping watch over the stray cows, Marcel, mind you,
endangered his own, his family's, fortune, yet he decided to run the risk.

"Citizens, a little child took charge of his neighbor! That's what it
amounted to. That was Marcel's great idea!

"You know the rest—how his friendly gesture not only saved all the
cows, but also turned out to be his own salvation, and, I might add, ours
too. Because that's what set us to thinking. It was an eye-opener to us.
We began to see that there is a better way of life than each man for
himself and the state for all. We began to see that if we would get
together of our own accord, life might be better in Monestier. And we
did get together, and one thing followed another, and here we are today,
celebrating, so to speak, the resurrection of our village. That's what it is—
the resurrection of our village. And the resurrection came from a child's

heart. That, citizens, is what we should not forget—ever. A little child led us." [52]

At the intermediate or junior high school level, the teacher could use *The Knights of King Midas* [53] by Paul Berna to help students see how the varied skills, capacities, talents, and energies of a group can be pooled and made to complement each other in the interests of a common economic goal. The huts of a group of elderly people have been burned down accidentally. The town clerk wants to take over the site on which the old people's homes were located. The old people have only a month to raise enough money to replace the temporary shacks in which they are living with modern dwellings. The elderly people's cause seems to be a lost one until eleven children decide to raise the money needed for new housing, a herculean undertaking. Each child eventually contributes something to the fund, by fishing, etc., and modern apartments are constructed in time.

And, at the senior high school level, the teacher might read aloud this now "classic" passage from the play *I Remember Mama* by John van Druten which shows a loving family's willingness to share the fruits of their labors and to sacrifice for each other in order to satisfy some of their most pressing economic needs and wants:

MAMA: Is all for this week. Is good. We do not have to go to the Bank.

.   .   .   .

NELS: Mama. . . . (*She looks up, catching an urgency in his tone.* PAPA *suspends smoking for a moment*) Mama, I'll be graduating from grammar school next month. Could I . . . could I go on to High, do you think?

MAMA (*Pleased*): You want to go to High School?

NELS: I'd like to . . . if you think I could.

MAMA: Is good.

(PAPA *nods approvingly*)

NELS (*Awkwardly*): It . . . it'll cost a little money, I've got it all written down.

.   .   .   .

MAMA: Get the *Little* Bank, Christine.

(CHRISTINE *gets a small box from the dresser*)

.   .   .   .

---

[52] From *All Alone*, by Claire Huchet Bishop, pp. 87-90. Copyright 1953, by Claire Huchet Bishop and Feodor Rajankowsky. Reprinted by permission of The Viking Press, Inc.

[53] New York: Pantheon Books, Inc., 1961.

NELS (*Anxiously*): Is there enough, Mama?

MAMA (*Shaking her head*): Is not much in the Little Bank right now. We give to the dentist, you remember? And for your roller-skates?

NELS (*His face falling*): I know. And there's your warm coat you've been saving for.

MAMA: The coat I can get another time. But even so . . . (*She shakes her head*)

CHRISTINE: You mean Nels can't go to High?

MAMA: Is not enough here. We do not want to have to go to the Bank, do we?

NELS: No, Mama, no. I'll work in Dillon's grocery after school.

(MAMA *writes a figure on the paper and starts to count on her fingers.* PAPA *looks over, and does the sum in his head*)

PAPA: Is not enough.

MAMA (*Finishing on her fingers against her collarbone*): No, is not enough.

PAPA (*Taking his pipe out of his mouth and looking at it a long time*): I give up tobacco.

(MAMA *looks at him, almost speaks, then just touches his sleeve writes another figure and starts on her fingers again*)

CHRISTINE: I'll mind the Maxwell children Friday nights. Katrin can help me.

(MAMA *writes another figure.* PAPA *looks over—calculates again, nods with satisfaction*)

MAMA (*Triumphantly*): Is good! Is enough! [54]

Having used literature to get at the idea of economic dependence and interdependence, the teacher might then invite his class to continue to uncover additional illustrations which are germane to the ongoing activities of the class. For example, a fifth grader reading the story of the Erie Canal might discover that lumber, grain, and meat products were the chief commodities to move eastward and that textiles, leather goods, machinery, hardware, and imported foods and drugs went west in exchange. The pupil could share this finding with his classmates, and, in time, our last economic generalization could be viewed from a number of sides. In the same way, an eleventh grade student in a United States history class might gain added feeling for the importance of economic interdependence upon uncovering this interesting statement written by Alexander Hamilton:

---

[54] Abridged from *I Remember Mama,* by John van Druten, pp. 13-16. Copyright, 1944, 1945, by John van Druten. Reprinted by permission of Harcourt, Brace & World, Inc.

An unrestrained intercourse between the States themselves will advance the trade of each by an interchange of their respective productions, not only for the supply of reciprocal wants at home, but for exportation to foreign markets. The veins of commerce in every part will be replenished and will acquire additional motion and vigor from a free circulation of the commodities of every part. Commercial enterprise will have much greater scope from the diversity in the productions of different States. When the staple of one fails from a bad harvest or unproductive crop, it can call to its aid the staple of another. . . .[55]

Finally, this last procedure designed to bring about some understanding of economic interdependence could be structured and adapted easily to any grade level. It would be a story in color slides of a given economic transaction and its wave of consequences. It should visualize for children and youth the point that individuals' economic lives touch each other in a very real way.

All of the pictures necessary for this method could be taken by the teacher on a single Saturday. He could use students, fellow teachers, or friends for "models" or "actors" in this economics drama; or he might find people at various places of business who would be willing to have their pictures taken. The slides might be as follows:

Slide 1: could show a husband and wife looking at the real estate section of the classified ads in their local newspaper and discussing their desire to purchase a nice residential lot on which to build a new home.
Slide 2: might deal with a real estate man showing a lot to the couple.
Slide 3: could have the real estate man conferring with the owner of the lot about an offer the couple has made on this piece of property.
Slide 4: could be of an attorney checking out the lot description, etc. for the couple.
Slide 5: could catch the attorney and his wife at the supermarket, buying groceries with part of the money he has received from the couple for his legal services.
Slide 6: could show the couple talking with a banker to make financial arrangements for the purchase of the lot.
Slide 7: might be a glimpse of the banker at lunch in a restaurant. His salary is paid by the bank from funds it receives for various services to people—like the couple he has helped.

---

[55] "Number 11," in Alexander Hamilton, James Madison, and John Jay, *The Federalist Papers* (New York: New American Library of World Literature, Inc., 1961), p. 89.

Slide 8: could show the former owner of the lot, purchasing a new car with the money he has received from the sale of his property.
Slide 9: might be of the real estate man buying a new suit with part of the commission he has received for selling the lot.

CONCLUSION

A quarter of a century ago, Kenneth Boulding wrote that "the task of economic analysis is to set before man as clearly as possible the alternatives among which he must choose." [56] This is still, in our opinion, a particularly terse and valid definition of a function of this interesting and important discipline. In the past, however, economics has had to live with the label "the dismal science" largely because of the gloomy alternatives it once offered concerning man's future on this earth. Today's economists are not necessarily as pessimistic, preferring to visualize a future of economic opportunity and well being, assuming that certain conditions are met.

In order for economic man to prosper, political man must, of course, learn to arbitrate and settle economic and other disputes in a manner that will assure human survival and the betterment of man's way of life. Similarly, an economic future of hope and promise depends upon our willingness to exchange knowledge and understanding for ignorance and superstition in our handling of man's economic affairs. Our schools and our teachers will have to recognize the need for an open-minded, non-restricted treatment of the economic world, rather than a program of narrow-minded indoctrination. Teachers, administrators, curriculum workers, school board members, and others will have to accept the notion that (as Wilbert E. Moore put it) "it is characteristic of . . . modern economic activity in general that it is constantly subversive of established ways, even its own, and entails a constant emphasis on change and improvement." [57]

We hope this book has succeeded in helping teachers to perceive some possibilities for the improvement of economic education at all grade levels as well as in acquainting them with teaching materials and techniques which might be used to implement their perceptions. We recognize, certainly, that no single volume can deal adequately with

---

[56] *Op. cit.*, p. 790.
[57] *Industrialization and Labor* (Ithaca, New York: Cornell University Press, 1951), p. 16.

a discipline as complex as economics, nor offer a complete program or curriculum designed to meet the needs of all children. On the other hand, we trust it will serve as an adequate prelude to additional study and experimentation.

Perhaps it is fitting that we close this volume with the words of one of the few truly innovative economic thinkers of our times, John Maynard Keynes. In 1945 Keynes delivered this toast before the Royal Economic Society in London:

> I give you the toast of the Royal Economic Society, of economics and economists, who are the trustees not of civilization, but of the possibility of civilization.

Index